University of Cambridge Department of Applied Economics

OCCASIONAL PAPER 36

# Do Trade Unions Cause Inflation?

**Two Studies: with a Theoretical Introduction
and Policy Conclusion**

# Do Trade Unions Cause Inflation?

## Two Studies: with a Theoretical Introduction and Policy Conclusion

Dudley Jackson
*Research Officer*
*Department of*
*Applied Economics*

H.A. Turner
*Montague Burton*
*Professor of*
*Industrial Relations*
*University of Cambridge*

Frank Wilkinson
*Research Officer*
*Department of*
*Applied Economics*

CAMBRIDGE

AT THE UNIVERSITY PRESS

1972

Published by
the Syndics of the Cambridge University Press
Bentley House, 200 Euston Road, London NW1 2DB
American Branch: 32 East 57th Street, New York, N.Y. 10022

© Department of Applied Economics, University of Cambridge, 1972


ISBN: 0 521 09788 6

Set by E.W.C. Wilkins Ltd., London,
and printed in Great Britain by Alden & Mowbray Ltd.
at the Alden Press, Oxford

# Contents

# Tables and graphs

**Section 3**

# 1. Introduction and theoretical note

(*H.A. Turner*)

The title of this Occasional Paper is not so much descriptive of its contents as provocative of them. In the phase of accelerated inflation in Britain from 1968 to 1972, probably by far the most widely-held view has attributed it to extravagant claims by trade unions. As authority for this view one could cite statements by leading politicians — from the Prime Minister down — by eminent academics, and by well-known journalists almost *ad infinitum*: and it has been particularly easy to find substance in it, because the period has also been one of remarkably intensified industrial unrest. At the close of the 1960's the British incidence of strikes rose from what was, by international comparison, a moderate level to one only previously rivalled in the great industrial conflicts that followed the First World War.

However, inflation has been going on for a long time — in many countries, for over thirty years — and both its recent acceleration and the parallel intensification of labour conflict are to some degree international phenomena. It has always been easy to regard unions as principal agents of the process, because wages appear to be adjusted mainly by a procedure of public confrontation: there are demands, counter-offers and rejections; bargaining occasionally breaks down, and the consequent stoppages of work cause public disturbance. However, the extent to which this procedure is even the main instrument by which wages rise is arguable.[1] And other incomes and prices are commonly adjusted by less public mechanisms: firms decide for themselves, in general and in the absence of a system of public price regulation, when and by how much their prices are to be changed; professional fees are sometimes automatically adjusted to changes in costs; and so on.

The publicity that attaches to formal wage determination is not therefore a sufficient reason for regarding it as the main source of inflation. And economists' views as to the responsibility of trade unions for persistently rising prices have in fact varied widely — from ones which ascribe them a negligible role to those which put the major blame upon them — and continue to do so. For instance, one might here refer to the strongly contrasting sense of Papers issued by two eminent economists under the imprint of the same rather notably non-radical Institute. Not so very long ago, one of them argued,

(1) The (now-defunct) British National Board for Prices and Incomes, for instance, estimated that between 1964 and 1666, about half the actual increase in average wage-earnings was accounted for by factors other than formally negotiated increases in wage rates (*Report No. 65*, 'Payment by Results Systems', H.M.S.O., London, 1968, para. 37).

1

in effect, that the historical relation (which comprised very different degrees of union strength at different periods) between the general rate of wage increase and unemployment was so determinate that it was only necessary to raise the latter to a sufficient (and rather moderate) level to control inflation. More recently, the other asserted that unions are not merely to be considered as monopolies, which like other monopolies raise their prices, but that they differ from other monopolies in continually attempting to do so; thus measures to restrain union strength, it would follow, are a prime necessity of inflation control. The first view was somewhat discredited by the recent coincidence, in the "industrial market" economies, of increased unemployment with accelerated inflation.[1] And the second view encounters the obvious difficulty that different rates of inflation, either between countries or historical periods, have not been clearly associated with differing relative strengths of trade unionism. But the notable thing is that two well-known economists of a similarly rather conservative tendency could have taken such opposite positions.

Economists who specialise in labour questions, and who know more about the specific matters at issue, would not generally be found in such extreme camps. Even so, their discussions of the influence of unions on the general level of money wages are far from having reached the degree of consensus achieved in relation to other aspects of wage-theory. Thus, most labour economists would agree that trade unions have a significant influence on wage-differentials: the difference is between those who think that influence generally subsidiary and those who consider it occasionally dominant. Similarly, few labour economists would say that unions can have no influence on the distribution of factor income — on labour's relative share in the economy's total product: nevertheless, very few indeed would ascribe their effect as comparable to, say, that of redistributive taxation. But where the impact of union organisation and pressure on the wage-level (and thus on prices) is concerned, the labour economists' discussion does not seem to have attained even that degree of focus.[2] Nor have the econometricians' studies — and there have been a considerable number of published statistical analyses of relative movements in wages, prices, employment and other variables in the last generation — brought matters to a decisive point, though this is no doubt partly due to the difficulty of giving statistical weight to such vaguely defined concepts as union strength or militancy, and as the influence of labour market policies or institutions.

It might, however, be useful to precede this Paper's subsequent analyses and discussion by at least attempting to put the issue in a formal framework

---

(1) It was in fact amended by post-script; whereupon yet another economist issued a paper through the same institute attempting to show that the increase in unemployment was not really real. For those who may be interested, incidentally, the various papers referred to above were published by the Institute of Economic Affairs, as *Hobart Papers* No. 29 and 47 (2nd Edition), *Readings in Political Economy* No. 6, and *Research Monograph* No. 28.

(2) This is partly, no doubt — and at any rate in Britain (though American labour economics seems in no better case, and few other countries have so far contributed much to the branch) — because of a preoccupation with micro-studies, which involve no such large speculations, and are thus safer.

of consideration. And this seems best done, following a well-established procedure in economic problem-solving, by seeing what would be likely to happen to the wage-level under certain very limited assumptions, and then progressively elaborating them (effects on the price-level being dealt with initially by supposing that changes in wage-costs per unit of output are proportionately reflected in prices).

Thus, suppose we first assume an economy: where the total supply of labour available for employment is fixed; in which there is something like a minimum wage for unskilled labour (which need not be an explicit one but may also be secured by, for instance, something like a "social minimum" — say an unemployment insurance or benefit below the level of which employers will find it difficult to hire labour, or even Marx's historically-determined "subsistence wage"); and in which there is a fairly perfect market (with free movement of workers and full information on wages and job opportunities) for skills.

Then the general supply curve for labour will be very much as in *Diagram A* — which states the relation between wages and the employment level. The general wage-level will be determined by that margin over and above the minimum wage which is just necessary to persuade workers to accept the extra personal costs of more responsible, dangerous or unpleasant work or of training for skills; and nobody will accept such work without that compensation. Equally, employers cannot hire unskilled labour below the "minimum wage"; nor can unskilled workers ask for more, while there are unemployed ones available. So the wage-level will not fall when employment is less than full. But when all the labour force *is* employed, the cost of hiring an additional worker is infinitely high, because no increase in wages can increase the labour supply. So the curve shifts abruptly at that point from a constant wage-level to one which rises indefinitely: it is right-angled.

But this is clearly unrealistic. For one thing, if *un*employment reaches a certain level, some of the existing skilled workers will prefer to accept jobs at less than the appropriate "skill margin" rather than compete with the unskilled for unskilled work; and if employment and economic activity fall low enough, the "minimum wage" will not hold (governments, for instance, will not be able to finance enough unemployment benefit). So the zone of stability in the wage-level will be limited in the direction of declining employment, and the labour supply curve will thereafter fall towards the origin (of no labour at no wages) as in *Diagram B*.

On the other hand, however (and this is more relevant to the present issue), it is never true that the labour supply is absolutely fixed, even in the very short run. Married women or retired people may be drawn back into the labour market by a rise in wages, for instance, and some of the primary labour force will work longer hours for overtime rates. And the effect is to replace the right angle in the labour supply curve by a slope near the point of full employment (described as *"Effect a"* in *Diagram B*). Moreover, workers are more willing to leave their present jobs when employment is high: labour turnover then increases, and employers will raise wages to hold their

(LSC = Labour supply curve)

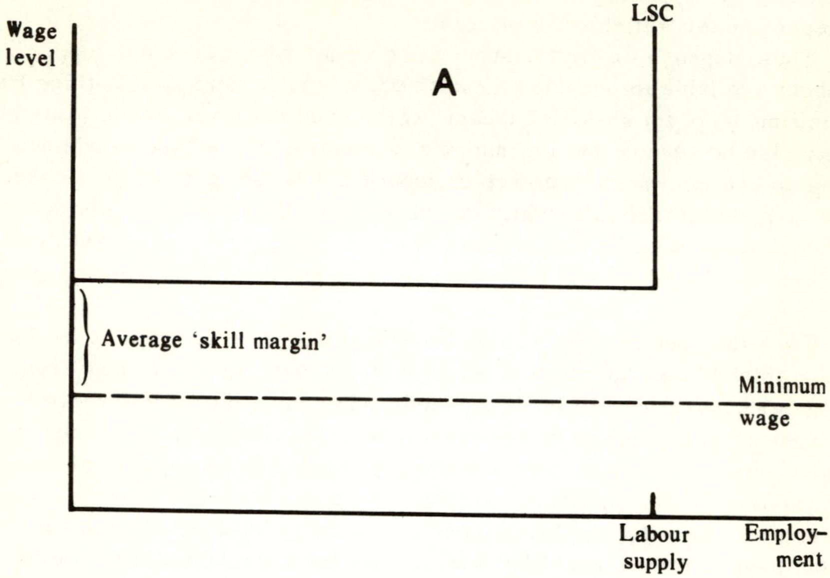


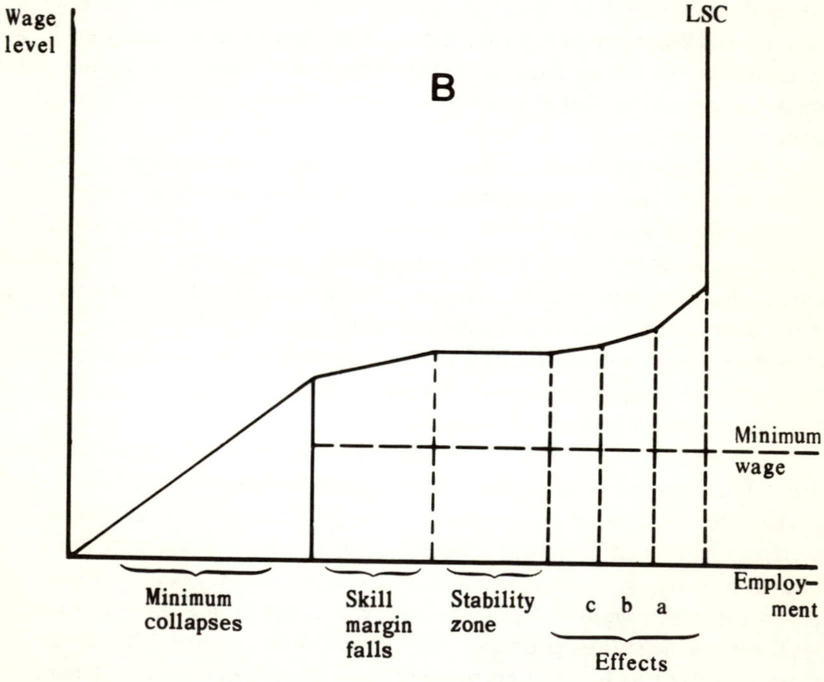

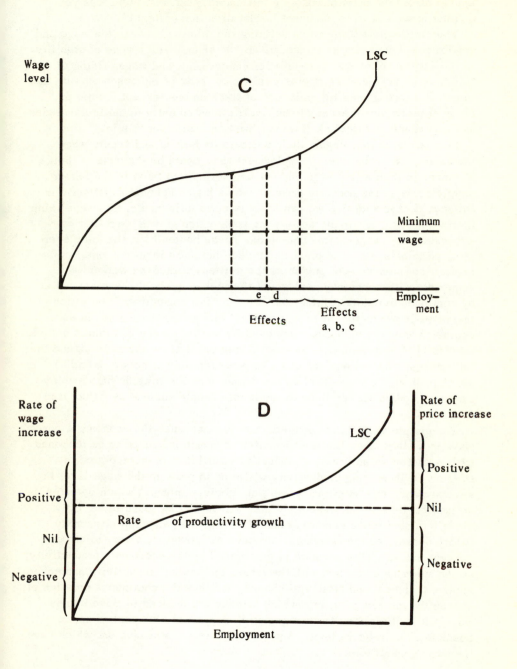

Diagrams A, B, C, D. The general labour supply curve (wage-increase/employment relationship) under various assumptions

employees, which puts a further slope into the curve (*Effect b*). And the labour market is in fact far from perfect: bottlenecks in the supply of skills appear before the point of absolute full employment, and this gives yet another upward twist to the curve in that direction (*Effect c*).

Thus in *Diagram B* the curve defining the relation between the wage and employment levels begins to assume an "S" shape, with a zone of stability in the wage level at a modest level of employment, and wages rising or falling at an accelerating rate as employment falls or increases outside that range. But this ignores the influence of trade unions (except insofar as union or professional associations' restrictions on entry to particular trades may contribute to *Effect c*). However, we can easily put this in.

In essence, unions enable their members to demand and secure wage increases at a lower level of employment than would be the case in their absence. So their effect is to add yet another upward twist to the labour supply curve as the economy moves towards high employment: *Effect d* in *Diagram C*. And with this we can associate the influence of the wage-fixing institutions that invariably accompany trade union growth — arbitration tribunals, legal wage-boards and so on. These bodies have two main operating principles, which in practice produce the same result:[1] one is that of implicit compromise — of producing the settlement that the workers and employers with whom they deal would themselves probably have arrived at by continued direct bargaining; the other is "fair comparison", by which increases in wages for these institutions' clients are determined in an approximate equity with those achieved by similar groups of workers outside their field of responsibility. So wage-fixing institutions virtually extend the influence of trade unions and of those other factors (*Effects a, b and c*) which push up the wage-level as the economy moves towards high employment: they add a further slope to the labour supply curve — as *Effect e* in *Diagram C*.

The picture is still not complete, however, because the economy it portrays is a static one. The most important dynamic influence to be reckoned with is that of steadily rising productivity, and this is incorporated in *Diagram D*. Increasing productivity will tend to push up the wage-level in several ways. The "minimum wage", or "social minimum" which operates as an implicit floor to the wage-structure, will in fact be found to be fairly closely related to the general standard of life in a particular community (which determines the meaning it attaches to "poverty", a very relative concept indeed). This standard is determined by the economy's productivity, so the minimum also rises with the latter. Increasing productivity, moreover, implies technical and structural change, and thus the continuous creation of new skills and new jobs, into which workers are induced to move by new wage-differentials; so the average "skill margin" is also pushed up, in absolute if not relative terms. And so on (there are other factors which have the same general effect).

(1) Cf. Turner: 'Arbitration: A Study of Industrial Experience', *Fabian Research Series*, No. 153, and 'Compulsory Arbitration in Britain' in *Research Paper* No. 8, Royal Commission on Trade Unions etc.

*Diagram D* allows for this dynamic influence by simply converting the "wage level" on the upright axis into the "rate of wage increase". The labour supply curve is still S-shaped, but the level of employment (or unemployment) now affects the rate at which wages on average change: their rate of increase accelerates as employment rises, but declines or becomes increasingly negative as employment falls.[1]

But we can now (at last) also incorporate a relation between wages and prices. If the hatched horizontal line in *Diagram D* represents the rate of productivity growth, we can read off the change in the economy's price level for any given rate of wage change by projecting the productivity line to another vertical axis, on the right, which measures price-movements. If wages are rising at the same rate as productivity, the price-level is stable. Prices on average rise when wage-increases exceed productivity growth, and fall when the rate of change in wages is less than or opposite to the increase of productivity.

This framework is not a mere logical exercise. The shape of *Diagram D*'s labour supply curve, would, for instance, be a pretty fair representation of the response of wages in Britain to changes in economic activity and employment in the present century. And specialists will recognise the curve's shape towards the right hand side of the diagram as approximating to that of the "Phillips Curve" — a now very well-known empirical formulation of the statistical record of that response over nearly a century.[2] But the framework also enables us to approach a number of problems in the theory of wages and inflation with more certainty. For instance, a recent controversy has centred on the question whether the Phillips Curve — which was originally interpreted as a new Iron Law of Wages — could change its shape or position, implying that the historical relationship between unemployment and the movement of wages could alter. The diagrams say, not merely that the position

(1) There is, of course, a two-way relationship here for, other things equal, the change in real wages (i.e. money wages re prices) relative to the change in productivity conditions — in a Keynesian sense — how the level of employment changes.

(2) Phillips, A.W. (of course) 'The Relation between Unemployment and the Rate of Change of Money Wages in the United Kingdom 1861—1957', *Economica*, Nov. 1958. (The 'Phillips Curve' embodied a statistical equation which implied only a gradually declining slope to the labour supply curve in the direction of low employment, but this may be because the occasions when unemployment was so high in Britain that wages fell sharply were too few to impact on the analytical procedure). There is now a vast and international literature of related and subsequent argument or statistical analysis (notable contributions to which have come — among scores of others — from G.C. Archibald, B. Corry with D. Laidler, J.C.R. Dow and L.A. Dicks-Mireaux, R.V. Eagly, O. Eckstein with T.A. Wilson, M. Friedman, A.G. Hines, C.C. Holt, N. Kaldor, E. Kuh, R.G. Lipsey, R.E. Lucas with L.A. Rapping, D.T. Mortensen, G.L. Perry, E.S. Phelps, A. Rees, J. Vanderkamp): which is mostly of conflicting effect. The 'framework' in this Introduction should be taken as one attempt to cut through the jungle of controversy, and present the matter's implications in terms which, hopefully, will be comprehensible to people operationally concerned with the actual economic relations and problems which are affected.

and slope of the general labour supply curve can change, but that it *has* changed, with the development of unions and institutional wage-fixing.[1]

Similarly, the framework enables us to say that the long-continuing controversy as to whether inflation is caused by "cost-push" or "demand-pull" is to some large degree unreal — or at least, is incorrectly formulated. What has happened, say the diagrams, is that the development of unions (and other factors) have pushed the point at which the general labour supply curve begins to rise sharply further down (or rather, to the left on) the employment scale. Wages will rise faster than productivity at a higher level of unemployment than was previously the case, because the shape of the curve has been changed. So inflation can be said to be due *either* to that change, *or* to the level of employment being too high to be consistent with price stability given the current supply curve for labour. Just as the inflation can be attacked *either* by reducing the demand for labour, *or* by attempting to push the labour supply curve back towards its previous position (for instance, by some form of deliberate wage-restraint or "incomes policy").

Moreover, the framework can also be adapted to deal with other complications in the inflation problem. For instance *Diagram D*, as formulated above, implies that the movement of the price-level is determined simply by the relation between the rates of change in productivity and in wages. But we know that wages also respond to changes in the price-level itself (at least, upwards). And we can take account of this by supposing — for instance — that the curve is defined in *real* wage terms, so that an independent upward pressure on prices will raise the whole curve proportionately. Thus, if prices are increasing at $x$ per cent autonomously (e.g. because the economy is experiencing deteriorating terms of external trade) the now rather narrow "stability zone" in the curve will correspond to a rate of wage increase equivalent to $x\%$ plus the average rate of productivity growth.

Or again, we can take in the effects of such things as changes in the distribution of factor income (i.e. in "labour's share"), or in the degree of monopoly. If the ratio of wages to profits *can* be changed by union pressure — and there is some agreement that this is at least possible under some circumstances[2] — then increases in wages relative to productivity (i.e., in unit wage-costs) will *not* be proportionately reflected in the price-level, and the price scale on the right-hand vertical of *Diagram D* will have to be adjusted accordingly. On the other hand, an increase in the degree of monopoly or oligopoly in the economy will have two effects: it will raise the price-level, which will feed back to the rate of wage-increase (as in the previous paragraph), at least as a temporary acceleration; on the other hand, it will raise profits in the sectors of the economy which are monopolized or oligopolised, and thus create more "room" for wage increases in those sectors, so that the slope of the labour supply curve will be twisted upwards yet again, and wage-inflation will commence at a still lower level of employment.

(1) This is a point that early exponents of the Phillips Curve analysis might themselves have appreciated sooner, had they known more about the unemployment and wage statistics they were using.

(2) Cf. E.H. Phelps Brown and Margaret Browne 'A Century of Pay' (Macmillan, London, 1968).

This last point introduces the very important consideration that the labour supply curve is by no means the only important price/activity relationship in the economy. Other supply curves — for instance, those for capital goods or for some agricultural products — may also steepen at a point well short of full capacity utilisation, so that prices of the goods or services concerned rise at an accelerating rate as the point of full employment is approached. The various curves are interrelated: and if the supply curve for a particular key commodity (like housing) happens to twist upwards sharply at an un- usually low level of capacity utilisation, implying that its price rises when unemployment is still substantial, this too will influence the labour supply curve in turn. Wage-inflation will again commence at a higher level of un- employment than would otherwise be so; but though this (to repeat) may be the most publicly-obvious aspect of the situation, that would certainly not in such a case be a reason to attribute primacy to wage-pressure as an in- flationary factor.

We can round off this preliminary theoretical exposition with one other point. This is that the normative relationship defined by *Diagram D* — that between the level of employment or unemployment and the rate of change in wages — is in the nature of a very general economic law. It no more says that a specified percentage of unemployment must automatically produce a particular rate of increase (or decline) in the wage-level than the law of gravity says that everything must fall down. Other local, specific or short- term factors intervene at particular moments of time,[1] and adjustments to these on either the wage or employment axis is not necessarily rapid. So actual positions in the employment-wage interraction will be found scattered around the curve. In particular, the Diagram's normative statement does not make it impossible for other broad cause-and-effect mechanisms (such as those indicated by this Paper's first study) to operate also: no more, again, than the law of gravity contradicts the laws of aerodynamics.

However, enough has perhaps been said to put the role of unions in in- flation into an initial perspective. There is clearly, if the foregoing dis- cussion is sound, a valid and important sense in which trade unions can be properly held to contribute to inflation. But they are only one of a number of factors which may equally do so, and the various factors are also highly intercorrelated. The problem therefore has to be redefined as one of the *relative* importance of various actors in the play, and of the degree of domi- nance to be attributed to one partner in an interconnected series of two-way relationships. But to solve this problem directly involves difficulties of measurement which seem, as yet, insuperable — we simply do not (as already noted) have data for several parameters one would need to include — and an almost intolerably complex structure of interrelations.

We therefore defer further consideration of that possibility to our conclusion. Meanwhile, the two studies that follow approach the problem indirectly — by attempting to answer certain questions which seem to have not yet been asked

(1) Including those of current 'expectations', on which see the opening to Section 2.

9

in the going controversy over inflation's causes and mechanisms, but which available evidence suggests to be extremely important. The first study takes a very broad view, and asks why inflations in the world as a whole should have concentrated, over the past two decades or so, into certain patterns, which are not merely economic but at the same time social, political and industrial. The other takes a rather narrower scope: nevertheless, it not merely examines the relationship of industrial unrest to inflation but asks just what it is (in an industrial economy like the British) that is to be considered as the "wage" around which union pressure and labour militancy are focussed. In the upshot, if we do not pretend to give a final and definitive solution to the initial question, we shall at least hope both to give it a closer definition and to limit the range of possible answers.

Some acknowledgements are due. The first study is in part based on and very much extends a paper published in *The Economic Journal* in December 1970;[1] some preliminary data of the second study was first briefly sketched in an article in *New Society*[2] of 25 February 1971 — from which, incidentally, a number of trade unions drew operational conclusions that (as this Occasional Paper's tailpiece may indicate) were somewhat the converse of those which were appropriate. In general, the material of the two studies is a by-product of other research enquiries. Data on wage and price-movements in many countries, and especially the Latin American material of the first study, were collected incidentally to an examination of labour problems in developing economies which was supported by the Overseas Development Administration: the first study's statistical examination of international links in inflation was also incidental to a survey of incomes policy problems financed by an anonymous foundation. In the second study, the problem of tax effects on wages was partly stimulated by an enquiry for which Mr. Wilkinson was a British Steel Corporation Research Fellow; and the connection with strikes is to some extent a residual product of research first supported by the Social Science Research Council. Our gratitude to these organisations makes the customary exemption of them from any responsibility for the result all the more emphatic in the present context. And the same exemption applies to the valuable assistance Mr. L.J. Handy, of the D.A.E., gave us at several points in these studies.

(1) "On the Determination of the General Wage Level: or 'Unlimited Labour Forever'" (Turner and Jackson).

(2) 'Real Net Incomes and the Wage Explosion' (Turner and Wilkinson).

# 2. Inflation, strato-inflation and social conflict

(*Dudley Jackson and H.A. Turner*)

### Theories of inflation

The variety of different policies currently being tried by governments in their efforts to control inflation is an ironic tribute not merely to the phenomenon's toughness and durability and to the fact that after thirty years' experience increasing public anxiety at continually rising prices should still be justified, but especially to the confusion caused by the large number of competing theories which purport to explain the origins and persistence of inflation.

Theories of inflation have the common characteristic that diverse policies of control based on them have so far not been very successful. But they can otherwise be classified into two broad groups: as either "monetary/expenditure" theories or as "structural/social" theories.

Monetary/expenditure theories range from simple propositions of the "too much money chasing too few goods" variety to sophisticated statements involving such superficially metaphysical notions as those of "a constant velocity of money" or "the real value of cash balances desired by the community".[1]  But in essence they all begin by describing the economy in terms of straightforwardly economic stocks and flows, and go on to explain inflation as resulting from some disequilibrium in the relationship between stocks and flows, or between flows and flows. This disequilibrium could, for instance, be the money stock rising relative to an income flow, or a money-expenditure flow rising relative to an output flow. Because of the large variety of stocks and flows in an industrial economy these theories of disequilibria can be elaborated to a considerable extent, depending on which variables and mechanisms the theoretician cares to emphasise.

The monetary/expenditure analysis, however, goes back to David Hume's essay *Of Money* in which he argued that an increase in the amount of gold

---

(1) Thus Milton Friedman ('Statement on Monetary Theory and Policy', reprinted in *Inflation*, ed. R.J. Ball and P. Doyle, Penguin, 1969) argues that while the individual can adjust his cash balance to any level he 'desires' the community as a whole cannot, and 'equilibrium' in a situation of full employment must be achieved by price changes: 'This essential difference between the situation as it appears to the individual, who can determine his own cash balances but must take prices and money income as beyond his control, and the situation as it is to all individuals together, whose total cash balances are outside their control but who can determine prices and money income, is perhaps the most important proposition in monetary theory.' pp. 141—2.

and silver in a country will first lead to an expansion of economic activity (because of the increased opportunities for profit), and eventually to a rise in prices, because it raises the price of labour. Hume argued from this that the optimal economic state was one of persistent mild inflation:

> The good policy of the magistrate consists only in keeping it [money], if possible, still increasing; because by that means he keeps alive a spirit of industry in the nation, and increases the stock of labour in which consists all real power and riches.[1]

Since 1741, Hume's "quantity theory" has been much elaborated, especially in terms of the "velocity of circulation", or a notionary equilibrium ratio between the money stock and the flow of output.[2] This monetary theory was, however, temporarily displaced by the rise of Keynesian economics, which concentrated attention upon the flows of expenditures arising from a "multiplier effect" of new ("exogenous") spending upon the initial base of total expenditure in the economy, and upon the "matching" flow of real output. This implied that an increase in the monetary flow without a corresponding increase in the flow of real output (because a state of full employment had been reached) would produce an 'inflationary gap' between the two flows which would be "filled" by rises in prices. More recent analysis has tended to conflate the two theories just referred to, by considering the role of credit in a modern economy: it being inferred that an expansion of the money supply which eases credit conditions will itself lead to an increase of exogenous expenditures, so causing inflation (or a balance of trade deficit) at full employment.[3]

The controversies around variants of these views are now becoming too arcane (and perhaps too subject to the law of diminishing fleas) to be worth pursuing any further here.[4] The essential point about monetary/expenditure theories is that, whatever the diagnosis, the policy prescription consists in changing some or other "relevant" and mainly fiduciary or fiscal variable, so that "equilibrium" may be restored. Basically inflation is seen simply as a *marginal* and almost wholly economic problem, requiring only appropriate monetary or fiscal measures (or a judicious mixture of both) to counteract it.

Structural/social theories of inflation stand in strong contrast, because they say that inflation arises from some *gross* imbalance in the economic,

(1) David Hume, *Essays Moral, Political and Literary* (Oxford University Press, London, 1963) p. 296.

(2) Milton Friedman and Anna Schwartz, *A Monetary History of the United States 1867—1960* (Princeton University Press, Princeton, 1963) explores this theme in great detail.

(3) *Committee on the Working of the Monetary System (The Radcliffe Report)* (H.M.S.O., London, 1959).

(4) The law referred to says that 'big fleas have little fleas upon their backs to bite 'em, little fleas have littler fleas, and so *ad infinitum*.' A detailed illustration of its application here is conveyed by H. Bronfenbrenner and F.D. Holzman, 'A Survey of Inflation Theory' in *Surveys of Economic Theory I* (Macmillan, London, 1965).

institutional or social structure, if not in some combination of the three. Such theories differ analytically among themselves in the source to which they attribute this imbalance: it may be regarded as due to continuing scarcities of particular key things such as food, foreign exchange, tax receipts; or it may be attributed more broadly to structural, quasi-monopolistic factors, such as deliberate restrictions on the supply of labour or commodities, the willingness of the political system to promote depreciations of the currency in the interest of particular groups,[1] and inequality in the ownership of capital and land. But these theories also have the common characteristic that the imbalance suggested does not lead (as it should in neo-classical economic theory) simply to a "once-for-all" adjustment of *relative* prices or incomes: groups which are adversely affected retaliate by attempting to raise their incomes also, and the process develops a "whip-saw" quality. Again such theories cover a range, including simple accusations (such as those that trade unions — or speculators — cause rising prices) and comprehensive condemnation (like the suggestion that inflation is a symptom of the general decay of capitalism). But they envisage the result of the original imbalance as a continuing inter-group conflict over the distribution of the social product.[2] These theories are therefore largely concerned not simply with the economic sources and mechanisms but also with the sociological dynamics of inflation.

Structural/social theories have received analytical attention mainly from development economists, beginning with the very significant observation by Aujac that "stocks and flows neither exist nor move by themselves", emphasising that the economy could *not* be seen simply as a set of abstract economic variables, but must be considered as a set of economic flows manipulated by the pressures of different social groups.[3] The theory was then expanded by a famous study of the peculiarities of inflation in Chile which suggested that Chilean inflation had its origin in the rigidity of food supplies, the slow growth of export earnings and the inflexibility of tax receipts — all of which were, however, linked with features of Chilean class, social and political organisation.[4] This paper emphasised the important distinction made above between such basic structural pressures as could start an inflation, and the social mechanisms which kept the inflation going. In the Chilean case, these mechanisms were defined in "the ability of

(1) See A.G. Ford, *The Gold Standard, 1880—1914: Britain and Argentina* (Clarendon Press, Oxford, 1962).

(2) Such theories have therefore appealed to those concerned to explain the distribution of income — cf. Nicholas Kaldor 'Alternative Theories of Distribution', in *Essays on Value and Distribution* (Duckworth, 1960), or Joan Robinson 'The Theory of Distribution', in *Collected Economic Papers* II (Blackwell 1960).

(3) Henri Aujac, 'Inflation as the Monetary Consequence of the Behaviour of Social Groups: A Working Hypothesis' *International Economic Papers* Number 4, 1954 (first published in French in 1950).

(4) Osvaldo Sunkel, 'Inflation in Chile: An Unorthodox Approach', *International Economic Papers Number 10*, 1960 (first published in Spanish in 1958).

different economic groups continually to readjust their real relative income": these groups, which could be historically identified, organised themselves in defence of their living standards and created various devices (devaluation, automatic cost-of-living adjustments to income etc.) to ease the social tensions created by inflation.

Theories of this type now have widespread acceptance in the Third World, because such structural imbalances and their social consequences are there very manifest. But "cost-push" theories of inflation in industrialised market economies belong to the same family of explanations. A cost-push theory is based on some one or combination of observed (or reasonably supposable) monopolistic and oligopolistic distortions or rigidities of the labour and product markets in such economies. Thus, in theories which emphasise trade union pressure and wage-inflation, the main underlying structural inflexibility is seen as relating to the supply of labour, and the social struggle for income shares takes place between unions and the rest of the community, between unions and oligopolistic industries, or perhaps as one of an implicit alliance of unions with oligopolists against other social groups.

Obviously such situations cannot be dealt with by marginal economic adjustments, such as changes in monetary policy. They require changes of major social institutions and attitudes. Stopping inflation is seen either as a problem of how to attack the position exploited by some formidably en-trenched and organised social group, or as a complex socio-economic and institutional problem requiring a broad range of policies with a wide cover-age of various imbalances.[1]

There are, of course, some propositions in the analysis of inflation which cut across the two groups of theories. Thus, the "Phillips Curve" — or rather, the family of curves (national, local, sectoral and modified)[2] which have trouped into the arena of economic discussion following Professor Phillips' first empirical formulation of a long-run relationship between changes in wages and unemployment for Britain — seems adaptable to theories of either type, though it was initially seized upon by monetary/expenditure proponents. And recently theories of both varieties have often been modified by an 'expectations' hypothesis. This says, in essence, that protracted experience of inflation will lead social groups, economic organisations and individuals to attempt to anticipate it — for instance, by increasing their income to compensate, not merely for past price increases but also for anticipated future increases, or by additional acquisitions of things which are likely to appreciate faster in cost. The effect of such actions is, of course, to in-crease the rate of inflation further — which makes attempts to anticipate it

(1) For instance: 'Inflation ... is a structural consequence of modern economic organisation which cannot be remedied except through structural or rather functional changes. It can be resolved through a profound alteration in the structural relationship between government, management and trade unions.' Thomas Balogh, *Labour and Inflation* (Fabian Tract 403, London, 1970), p. 41.

(2) Edmund S. Phelps *et. al.*, *Microeconomic Foundations of Employment and Inflation Theory* (Macmillan, London, 1971).

still more likely, and so on.[1] Such expectations hypotheses have recently been incorporated into theories of inflation, largely in an attempt to explain why the rate at which prices rose should have accelerated sharply in many countries around 1969 or 1970, despite a general increase in unemployment and in surplus industrial capacity which was to a large degree engineered by governments in an attempt to stop wages and prices rising.

However, these qualifications do not obliterate the basic difference between the two main families of inflationary theory. The first type of theory, involving only relatively marginal adjustments to monetary and expenditure variables, has the great apparent advantage of political simplicity, which is invaluable to politicians who have to propagandise and explain the policies they wish to apply. It appears to offer a method of dealing with rising prices 'at a stroke' without too great government intervention in the economy or selective disturbance to vested interests. But the disadvantage is that, to the extent that the second, structural/social group of theories also contains elements of truth, the cost of the implied deflationary policies in terms of unemployment, wasted productive capacity and social conflict may be unacceptably high. This has been long noted for both the less developed and the industrialised market economies.[2] But such theories (or at least their more simplistic forms) have become particularly suspect in the light of the recent experience of intensified inflation combined with wide-spread capacity under-utilization.

The structural/social type of theory has the operational-theoretical advantage of distinguishing between 'basic' causes and propagation mechanisms, and might well seem more 'realistic' to a public now wearied by long experience of 'freezes', 'squeezes' and their consequential sectional resistances and frictions. But the disadvantage of this type of theory is that it makes it extremely difficult, both technically and politically, for any government without absolute power to devise and to maintain policies which will in fact control inflation. According to the particular variety of theory which is adopted or assumed, the structural reconstitution implied will involve either a direct confrontation with a major (and necessarily powerful) social group, or a complex, arduous and persistent co-operation between such social groups and the state, in which much is unknown or experimental but in which also any false step or important case of sectional evasion and backsliding may provoke disaster and disillusionment.

Discussion of alternative theories is thus also complicated because the different varieties are also often heavily orientated politically. It is important, however, that the division between the two families does not necessarily correspond to 'right and left'. Broadly speaking, monetarists are against

(1) See for instance, Sir John Hicks 'Expected Inflation', *Three Banks Review*, September 1970.

(2) E.g. Bronfenbrenner and Holzman, *op. cit.*, 'Fiscal and monetary policies ... may cure a cost inflation only at the price of unemployment and slower growth ...' p. 47.

'planning', but expenditure theories have also been espoused by labour or radical groups (e.g. in the statements that inflation is not due to the unions but to military spending or financial speculation). Supporters of 'cost-push' theories commonly advocate 'incomes policies', but these may be indentified with socialist economic planning, *or* with anti-union measures in an otherwise *laisser-faire* economy.

As a matter of historical explanation, we do not think it possible to make an *a priori* choice between either group of theories. There is clearly something in both of them. The modern inflation in the industrial countries dates back, in essence, to the competitive rearmament spending which immediately preceded World War II;[1] and before that, individual national inflations were sometimes obviously caused by large government expenditures, lack of monetary control, and loans or fiscal favours to particular social groups. Many present-day national inflations were probably *initiated* by monetary excesses; and inflation *could* be stopped by sufficiently severe monetary or credit restraint.[2] Similarly, there are obviously cases where inflation has been set off by large wage or price increases, such as Lumumba's doubling of the Congolese legal minimum wage; and inflation has often been stopped temporarily by wage-price freezes, or even suppressed over a run of years by draconic state controls (as in Hitler's Germany). At this point in the discussion, however, it seems important to recognise two things. One is the distinction between basic causes and propagating/perpetuating mechanisms. The other is — in any case — the inevitability that a world social phenomenon with as broad consequences as persistent inflation should have become, after over thirty year' endurance, a very complex affair, with multiple mechanisms involving forces which have become virtually independent of the Original Sin, and which no simple theory could now completely embrace.

We are for this reason (among others) less concerned to criticise existing theories than first to state two basic facts about inflation that none of the

(1) It seems to us that many of the socio-economic origins of modern inflation are to be found in the conditions of the Second World War itself, and that many of the phenomena we shall be discussing can be seen clearly in the war economies. During the War, full employment of labour and capital became the norm, and a condition of suppressed inflation was quite evident. In Britain monetary and fiscal policy was very carefully regulated; inflationary shocks were curtailed by socially acceptable, indeed socially demanded, rationing and subsides; while wages and industrial relations were (after some initial difficulties) judiciously handled. But all this would be another story: see, A.J. Brown, *The Great Inflation 1939–1951* (Oxford University Press, 1955) and the following histories of the Second World War: R.S. Sayers, *Financial Policy 1939–1945* (H.M.S.O., 1956); W.K. Hancock and M.M. Gowing, *British War Economy* (H.M.S.O., 1949); and H.M.D. Parker, *Manpower: A Study of War-time Policy and Administration* (H.M.S.O., 1957). It is also significant in this regard that the (direct) basis of the macro-economic theory of inflation is J.M. Keynes' booklet *How to Pay for the War* (Macmillan, 1940).

(2) Although the monetarists perhaps underestimate the difficulties of controlling the money supply: in the Irish bank strike of 1970, the supply of bank money and credit was cut off for six months without important effect on the economy. If there isn't enough money, people are quite capable of creating their own!

theories appear even to have noted. Until an explanation of these major
facts is incorporated, any theory must stand condemned for its inadequacy.
The lesser of these facts is that (to date, at any rate) the pace of inflation
in the world at large has in the long run not accelerated, but has oscillated
around a relatively steady path. And the greater of these facts is that
national average rates of inflation have not been spread over a spectrum, but
have fallen into distinct clusters, which have been maintained over lengthy
periods. Our following major purpose is to account for these two dominating
facts.

## Some facts

On the 'expectations' hypothesis, inflation should accelerate indefinitely,
because as more and more people adjust their expenditure or income claims
to anticipate a continuation of rising prices, the latters' upward movement
is itself accentuated — which in turn leads to still more emphatic attempts
to anticipate future inflation. And such an acceleration is certainly the
implication of structural/social theories in general: whatever initiates the
inflationary curve, any initial sectional gain will be at least partially
cancelled by the reaction of other groups. As the initiating group attempts
to restore its first advantage (which it may now regard as an established
right) still other groups will organise to defend their relative positions, so
the general pace of inflation is further speeded up. The ultimate point
would be reached when every social group both was organised and possessed
an automatic and immediate adjustment (or 'indexisation') of income, not
merely to prices, but to changes in *per capita* money income at large — when
inflation would necessarily occur at an infinitely explosive rate.

But no such long-run tendency to acceleration is exhibited by the world
historical record. Graph I shows the average annual increase in consumer
price indices (i.e. retail prices weighted by their importance in consumption)
for the 81 non-communist economies for which this data is available from 1948 to
1971.[1] In the light of this, the movement from 1968 to 1971, which has
caused so much concern in many countries, appears a comparatively normal
oscillation: it was considerably smaller than the 1950/51 upsurge, and
exceeded by those of 1955/56 and 1962/64. And though in the industrial
countries particularly, the rate of inflation accelerated more than in economies
of other types, even there the peak was considerably lower, on average, than
that of 1951.

(1) Source, United Nations, *Statistical Year Book* and *Monthly Bulletin of Statistics*
    plus local sources for certain countries for which the international record is
    incomplete; year-to-year percentage changes being calculated for each country,
    with estimates for certain countries where there were interrupted series in
    particular years, and simply averaged arithmetically over the whole. The Graph
    is thus an (unweighted) average of all available rates of change in national
    consumer price indices, with the exception of those for a very small number of
    Asian countries where the price record was irretrievably distorted by wars or
    similar events. An unweighted average is used because of our concern with the
    average experience of individual countries.

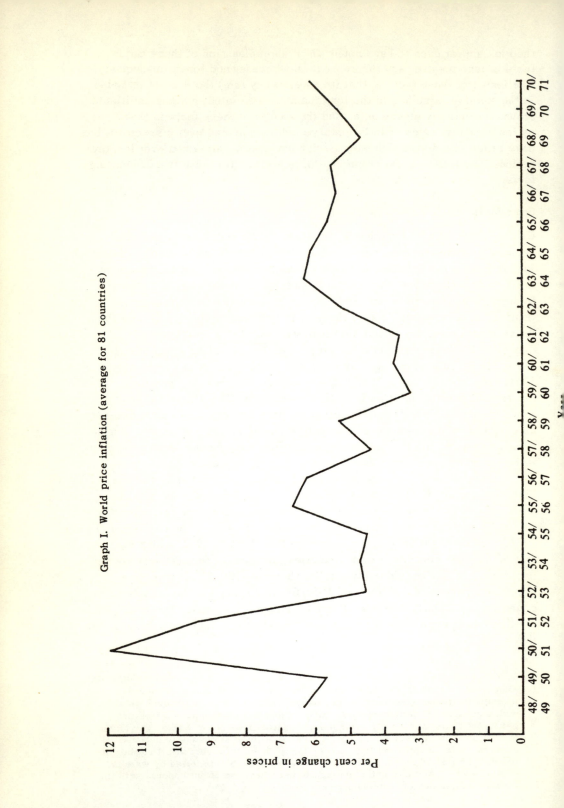

Graph I. World price inflation (average for 81 countries)

Per cent change in prices

Year

Table 1. *Average annual rates of consumer price inflation*
*by groups of countries*

| 5-year periods Countries | 1948/53 | 1953/58 | 1958/63 | 1963/68 | 1968/71[a] |
|---|---|---|---|---|---|
| Industrialised (19) | 6.0 | 2.7 | 2.5 | 4.0 | 5.3 |
| African (18) | 8.9 | 2.9 | 2.1 | 3.8 | 4.0 |
| Asian (12) | 3.0 | 1.7 | 1.7 | 3.2 | 4.2 |
| Mediterranean (9) | 4.7 | 4.9 | 3.4 | 3.8 | 5.2 |
| Latin American[b] (22) | 11.3 | 11.7 | 9.0 | 11.1 | 7.0 |
| Latin American[b] (excluding[c]) (16) | 4.8 | 2.6 | 2.6 | 3.3 | 3.8 |

[a] 3 years only.

[b] Includes Caribbean.

[c] Bolivia, Brazil, Chile, Argentina, Paraguay, Uruguay.

Considering the recent period in more detail, the years 1968 to 1971
again appear in no way out of line with post-war historical experience
(Table 1). The justification for separating certain Latin American countries
in Table 1 will appear immediately. Otherwise, the picture it presents for
particular 5-year periods depends on the timing of the series' peaks and
troughs. But there has fairly clearly been, apart from these two considerations, a tendency for the world rate of inflation to vary around 3 or 4 per
cent annually.

True, there is some evidence that the various peaks in this historical
fluctuation were associated with successively higher levels of unemployment, which gives some weight to the suggestion that the general force of
inflationary pressures was increasing over the whole post-war period. On
the other hand, preliminary data for 1972 suggests that even in the industrial
countries the curve of inflation was turning down towards its normal path:[1]
in several such countries, the rate at which prices rose had already slackened
in 1971 itself. (It is perhaps of some relevance to recent economic events
in Britain that only two 'industrial' economies, the United Kingdom and
Ireland, show a repeated annual acceleration in the rate of inflation over the
whole period 1966 to 1971; but even in Britain the rate fell substantially in
1971–72).

It would be hazardous to project incomplete recent data into the future.
And our later argument may well imply that since 1968 several countries have
moved from a moderate inflationary state to the brink of a more explosive
variety, and that the forces confining inflation in general to a moderate path

(1) Thus for 19 industrial 'market' economies for which data is, at time of writing,
available, average price trends run (per cent annual increase):

| 1966/67 | 1967/68 | 1968/69 | 1969/70 | 1970/71 | 1971/72 (Apr.–Apr.) |
|---|---|---|---|---|---|
| 3.5 | 3.8 | 4.4 | 5.6 | 6.0 | 5.9 |

Incidentally, the apparent unusual acceleration of inflation shown for
'Mediterranean' countries in Table 1 over 1968/71 is mainly due to the inclusion
of Turkey.

may recently have been significantly weakened. But so far nothing funda-
mentally contradicts our picture, for the world as a whole and for broad
groups of economies — if not for all individual countries — of an inflation
which has been persistent but contained, though perhaps at an increasing
cost.

Our second — and possibly more important — fact, however, concerns
the distribution of countries by their particular average annual rates of
inflation. Setting aside for the moment the 'expectations' hypothesis — if
only as not yet made fully consistent with the world evidence — monetary/
expenditure theories would seem to imply that individual countries would
be found scattered over a wide range of inflation rates, from nil to infinite,
according to their respective degrees of monetary/fiscal discipline and
control. And something of the same distribution might be expected from
structural/social theories, since individual national inflation rates would
depend upon the degree and kind of particular countries' structural
imbalance, the date at which this induced an initial inflationary push, the
extent of retaliatory organisation by social groups or of 'mutual indexisation', and so on. But no such distribution appears from the record.

Our Graph II includes, as well as the 81 countries already referred to, 7
further communist economies.[1] The histogram shows that individual
countries have fallen into three quite distinct clusters, so far as their
price experience is concerned. The communist countries, with one exception,
fall close to zero inflation. Most other countries are distributed around a
modal rate of 3 per cent annually, with a small inter-country variance.[2]
Then there is an entirely separate cluster around the 30 per cent rate, but
with a largeish inter-country variance. No theory to date has observed this
'cluster' effect, and the discontinuity between the latter clusters. Nor would
any such theory appear to provide a basis for explaining it, although it is
obviously a major feature of post-war inflation.

On the communist countries, we refrain from much comment. Excluding
Yugoslavia, those for which data is available have an average long term
rate of price inflation of *minus* 0.4 per cent per annum, and so form a separate
category of experience. There is some dispute as to the validity of official
price indices for the communist countries,[3] but we are not ourselves

(1) Again the distributions within 5-year periods were not dissimilar to that shown
by the 1948–71 histogram, and Table 1 shows that nothing really out-of-the-way
has happened recently. Data for the communist economies runs only from 1953,
however. It should also be noted that the analysis again excludes certain
countries where, because of war, revolution or some parallel upheaval, price
series were radically disrupted: but we will refer to these later.

(2) Which is, incidentally, probably somewhat exaggerated by the differing composition and structure of national price indices.

(3) In addition to American criticisms, the official Russian Price Index has recently
been under attack from Russian statisticians. See Michael Ellman's review of
the late Professor A.L. Vainshtein's book on the national income of Russia and
the U.S.S.R., *Naroanyi dokhod Rossii i SSSR*, in *Soviet Studies*, April 1970,
pp. 526–7.

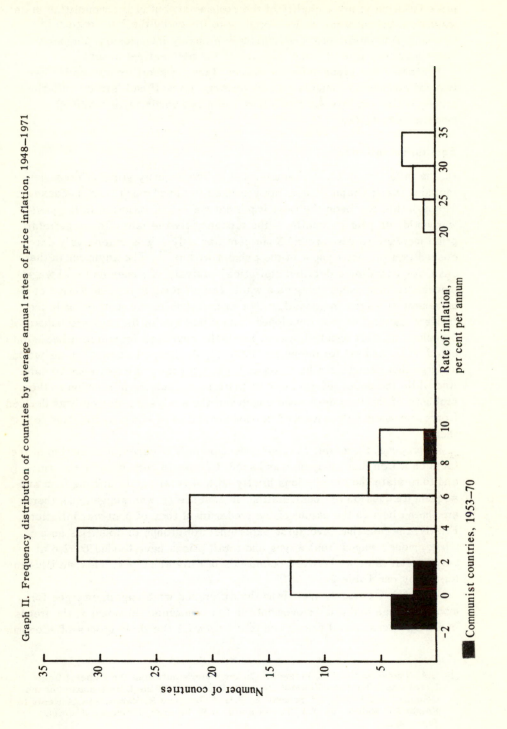

Graph II. Frequency distribution of countries by average annual rates of price inflation, 1948–1971

Number of countries

Rate of inflation, per cent per annum

■ Communist countries, 1953–70

disposed to regard this as substantially modifying their distinctness. Zero price inflation is not a quality of the communist, but of the monolithic state: wages and prices were, as we noted, also frozen by the Nazi regime in Germany. And *democratic* communism is probably inflationary: Yugoslavia has a long-term rate of price inflation of 9.2 per cent per annum.

Otherwise, we propose for the moment (and for short) to categorise our two non-communist clusters as categorising 'normal' and 'strato' inflations respectively, and proceed to discuss these two empirically-observed varieties separately.

### Equilibrium inflation

On the inflation which is characterised by the majority group of countries included in our Graph II, it is not proposed to spend much time, because although this has been the most important variety of inflation in the post-war world, its primary quality — the tendency for the rate of average retail price increase to vary around 3 per cent annually — was extensively discussed in a previous paper of the present writers.[1] The argument in that case was based on a detailed statistical analysis of money and real wage movements in manufacturing as a whole (as reasonably representative of the movement of wages in general, either in industrialised countries or in the 'modern sectors' of less developed economies) and in its separate industrial branches, as well of retail prices, in all the countries for which reliable data could be assembled for the period 1956—65. As Graph I shows, for the world at large that decade can be taken as typifying post-war experience to date. And while the paper referred to was written particularly in relation to the problems of the less developed countries, the analysis it set out was derived from comparison with advanced economies and is of equal application to them.

We propose, therefore, in this connection only to repeat a selection of the facts on which that analysis was based, to refer to certain later material, and to re-state the conclusions briefly with several points arising from subsequent discussion or consideration. In essence (it was suggested), there are three clues to the nature of the predominant form of post-war inflation. Firstly, the fact that, averaging experience for groups of countries as a whole, money wages, real wages and retail prices have tended to rise at very similar rates as between economies of different types. This we illustrate tersely by our Table 2.

As is fairly evident, apart from the difference which again emerged for monetary wage and price movements in the communist economies, the trends in money wages, retail prices and real wages for the three groups of economies

---

(1) H.A. Turner and D.A.S. Jackson: 'On the Determination of the General Wage Level, etc.' *Economic Journal*, loc. cit. See also 'On the Determination of the General Wage Level: A Comment' by J.B. Knight and R. Mabro, and 'A Reply to Knight and Mabro', by H.A. Turner and D.A.S. Jackson, *Economic Journal*, June 1972.

Table 2. *Changes in wages and prices by groups of countries, 1956–65*[a]

(% increase p.a.)

| Mean of Country Averages for | Money Wages | Prices | Real Wages |
|---|---|---|---|
| 19 Advanced 'market' economies | 6.4 | 3.0 | 3.3 |
| 4 'Planned' economies | 4.4 | 0.6 | 3.8 |
| 32 Less developed economies | 6.6 | 3.4 | 3.3 |

*Sources, and detailed descriptions:* see Turner and Jackson 'On the Determination of the General Wage Level, etc.' *loc. cit.* In the original paper, data is also given separately for more restricted groups of economies, within which the data available is more satisfactory for certain statistical purposes. For such groups the *general* results represented above are, however, statistically identical. But the results for the small group (originally five) of 'planned' economies were heavily distorted by the notable Yugoslav diversion to which we have already referred: with Yugoslavia included, that group's averages became:

| % increase p.a. | Money Wages | Prices | Real Wages |
|---|---|---|---|
| 5 'planned' economies | 7.3 | 2.5 | 4.7 |

[a] Note that Table 2 also now excludes three 'strato-inflationary countries', Argentina, Brazil and Chile, for reasons perhaps already sufficiently evident.

were then found to be statistically identical (i.e. the small differences between average wage and price movements in the advanced and less developed countries as groups did not prove significant on statistical tests, and no significant difference in average *real* wage trends was found between the three groups of countries). It was noted that the trend of real wages corresponded closely to the average trend of productivity growth within the separate groups — i.e. for productivity in industrial (and 'planned') economies, as well as in the modern sector of less developed ones, to rise at about 3½ per cent a year.[1]

There have, however, been substantial variations between the separate experiences of individual countries within each *group*. And there are, particularly, often significant variations between the rate of wage increase in individual industries within each *economy*. Both of these variations have been less pronounced for the industrial than the less developed economies, but the important point (and our second clue to the mechanics of 'normal' inflations) is that differences in the rate of wage increase between industries appear systematic. Wages have apparently tended to rise faster in capital-intensive oligopolistic industries with relatively high rates of productivity growth.

Since our analysis was made, much more definitive evidence both as to the positive connection between the respective dispersals of productivity growth rates and rates of wage increase among industries in advanced countries, and as to the consequences of those dispersals' difference, has

(1) For some discussion of the evidence, see 'Comment' by Knight and Mabro, and 'Reply' by Turner and Jackson, *loc. cit.*

been uncovered by the work of Messrs. Eatwell, Llewellyn and Tarling:[1] which is to be published, so we say no more of it here. But our third clue is the evidence, of which again we cite an extract in the *Matrix* of our Table 3, that, comparing individual countries (in this case, including both industrialised and less developed ones) the dispersal of wage increase rates between industries *within* an economy has been inversely connected with particular countries' degree of general wage and price inflation – so that the more equal were wage-advances in different industries, the higher the national rate of inflation has tended to be. And the *Matrix* of Table 3 also shows that the dispersal of wage increases in individual countries was inverse to two measures (here called the 'inter-industry linkage of wage increases' and the 'stability of inter-industry wage structure') of the degree of integration, whether economic or institutional, in national labour markets.

These three clues were in effect associated with a well-known and empirically founded proposition in the theory of market oligopoly – that of the 'kinked product demand curve': which in effect says that in industries whose product markets are dominated by a few big firms, individual concerns (though each may fear that an autonomous *increase* in product prices would switch demand to its competitors) will be reluctant to reduce prices because they do not believe that such action will transfer enough consumers' allegiance from their competitors' products to compensate for the loss of revenue.[2] This proposition was first derived to explain why competition between oligopolistic enterprises should take other forms than price reductions. But in the present context it would also explain why industries which were both oligopolistic and had (for technical or economic reasons) high productivity growth rates should be willing to accede to union demands for wage increases going beyond the *national* average rate of productivity growth. They prefer in effect, to increase wages beyond that average rather than reduce their prices.

But if wages in industries where productivity growth is naturally high are regularly raised in step with sectoral productivity, it is inevitable that there will be pressure in other industries to raise wages in line – either from the workers of those industries themselves, or from employers' competition for labour. And in those other industries, this will inevitably lead to price increases. Suppose, for instance, that productivity growth in the leading

---

(1) 'Industrial Wage Inflation', Department of applied Economics, July 1972 (mimeo). As we understand it, these Cambridge analysts' result refers statistically only to the connection of productivity and wage increase rates. However, we take the association of high productivity growth with capital intensity and oligopoly to be inferrable.

(2) W.A.H. Godley and C. Gillion ('Pricing Behaviour in Manufacturing Industry', *National Institute of Economic and Social Research, Economic Review*, Aug. 1969) also found that price changes in engineering products were unsymmetrically distributed, implying that even if unit costs were on *average* constant, firms would be more willing to increase particular prices than to reduce others. This would, of course, have the same effect on wages as oligopoly.

Table 3. *Matrix of wage and price relationships (all non-Communist countries)*

| | Money wages, rate of increase | Retail prices, rate of increase | Real wages, rate of increase | Money wages, irregularity of increase | Money wages, inter-industry dispersal of annual increases | Money wages, inter-industry dispersal of growth rates | Wages levels, inter-industry inequality | Inter-industry 'linkage' of wage increases | Stability of inter-industry wage structure |
|---|---|---|---|---|---|---|---|---|---|
| Money wages, rate of increase | | ++ | ++ | = | = | = | | ++ | |
| Retail prices, rate of increase | | | | | | | | | |
| Real wages, rate of increase | | | | | | | | | |
| Money wages, irregularity of increase | | | | | ++ | ++ | ++ | = | |
| Money wages, inter-industry dispersal of annual increases | | | | | | ++ | ++ | = | = |
| Money wages, inter-industry dispersal of growth rates | | | | | | | ++ | = | = |
| Wage levels, inter-industry inequality | | | | | | | | = | = |
| Inter-industry 'linkage' of wage increases | | | | | | | | | ++ |
| Stability of inter-industry wage structure | | | | | | | | | |

Correlations and Significance (Two Tail Test)

| | Positive | Negative |
|---|---|---|
| | To 5% level: ++ | To 5% level: = |

*Source:* See Turner and Jackson, 'On the Determination of the General Level of Wage Level, etc.', *loc. cit.* Note that the number of countries covered (30) is less than in Table 2, because of the non-availability of adequate data on wages by industry in other cases.

(or 'key') industries averages 7 per cent annually, and wages there rise by the same amount. Productivity growth rates in other industries being assumed to be spread normally from zero to 7 per cent annually, then the *average* rate of price inflation will depend on the extent to which their workers' wages keep up with those in the leading industries. If wages in all industries move quite in line, at 7 per cent p.a., and since *average* productivity growth is 3½ per cent annually, prices will also rise at 3½ per cent — as will real wages.[1] These figures are very close to those of our Table 2.

(1) The model implicit in this analysis can be put more formally as follows, where: $w$ = average money earnings; $v$ = value added per employee at constant prices; $p$ = price index; $V$ = total value added; $a$ is a parameter. Then for the $i$th sector, where * denotes the 'key' wage increase and ⁻ denotes the economy wide average:

$$\left(\frac{\Delta w}{w}\right)_i = a_i \left(\frac{\Delta w}{w}\right)^* \tag{1}$$

but as

$$\left(\frac{\Delta w}{w}\right)^* = \left(\frac{\Delta v}{v}\right)^* \tag{2}$$

$$\left(\frac{\Delta w}{w}\right)_i = a_i \left(\frac{\Delta v}{v}\right)^* \tag{3}$$

also

$$\left(\frac{\Delta p}{p}\right)_i = \left(\frac{\Delta w}{w}\right)_i - \left(\frac{\Delta v}{v}\right)_i = a_i \left(\frac{\Delta v}{v}\right)^* - \left(\frac{\Delta v}{v}\right)_i \tag{4}$$

therefore

$$\left(\frac{\overline{\Delta p}}{p}\right) = \Sigma \left(\frac{\Delta p}{p}\right)_i \frac{V_i}{V} = \Sigma \left\{ a_i \left(\frac{\Delta v}{v}\right)^* - \left(\frac{\Delta v}{v}\right)_i \right\} \frac{V_i}{V} \tag{5}$$

$$= \left(\frac{\Delta v}{v}\right)^* \Sigma a_i \frac{V_i}{V} - \left(\frac{\overline{\Delta v}}{v}\right)$$

Equation (1) states that the wage increase in sector $i$ will be some fraction, $a_i$, of the 'key' sectoral increase. The coefficient $a_i$ allows for the fact that lagging sectors might not be able to keep up with the advancing sectors, $a_i < 1$ (or, indeed may exceed its increase in an attempt to return to an absolute differential so that $a_i > 1$). Equation (2) is our postulate that the 'key' rate of wage increase is equal to productivity growth in the sector of fastest growth of productivity. From which it follows that the wage increase in the $i$th sector is some fraction of the fastest rate of productivity advance. Equation (4) states that the rate of price inflation in the $i$th sector is the difference between the rate of wage increase and the rate of productivity advance in that sector. Therefore, equation (5), the rate of economy-wide price inflation, is the sum of sectoral rates of price inflation, weighted by their share in total value-added, so that the average rate of inflation is equal to some fraction of the maximum rate of productivity increase minus the average rate of productivity increase. If all the $a_i = 1$, then the average rate of price inflation is simply equal to the difference between the rate of growth of productivity in the most rapidly advancing sector and the average rate of productivity growth. If the labour market is not well integrated and $a_i < 1$, for all or most sectors, the rate of price inflation will be lower.

This analysis may be regarded as a dynamic version of a static theory which has a long history. [1] In our initial paper we also included the effect of international competition as an additional regulator of the model, as limiting the extent to which individual countries could depart from the pattern of persistent and regular inflation it implied; but this aspect is one which we now intend to elaborate somewhat, and so defer consideration of it or the moment. However, we can note here that a national study by three authors professionally associated with the working of the Swedish labour market gives strong support to the type of dynamic intersectoral model implied in our analysis, and also extends the model to encompass the international constraints on domestic price inflation. [2] This latter study divides the Swedish economy into an internationally competitive sector and a 'sheltered sector'. In the former sector, productivity growth is 7.5 per cent annually (1960–1967), in the latter 3.0 per cent. [3] But, 'the competitive sectors, especially industry, have been wage leaders for a long time' [4] and wages throughout the economy have gone up at 8 per cent to 9 per cent annually; the extra percentage point added to wage increases being made possible because of the 'room' provided by an increase in relevant international prices of about 1 per cent annually. [5] These wages movements necessitated price increases in the low productivity growth, sheltered sector of 5.6 per cent per annum. [6] Sweden thus appears as a special case of our own model in which a rather high national productivity growth rate has both induced a slightly faster than average inflation and — in association with an advantageous export specialisation — made it tolerable.

Given the continuity of productivity growth (which is largely conditioned by technology) and the structural stability of the labour market, our 'normal' rate of inflation will continue at a fairly steady pace, real wages will also rise steadily, and the system will continue in 'equilibrium' as long as growth

(1) Bronfenbrenner and Holzman, *op. cit.*, pp. 68 ff., give the details. Also see the somewhat neglected Essays 5, 6, and 7 by Sir John Hicks in *Essays in World Economics* (Clarendon Press, Oxford, 1959).

(2) G. Edgren, K-O. Faxén and C-E. Odhner, 'Wages, Growth and the Distribution of Income', *Swedish Journal of Economics*, September 1969. (The authors are not academics but are economists with the Swedish Central Organisation of Salaried Employees, the Swedish Employers' Confederation, and the Swedish Confederation of Trade Unions respectively. Perhaps this explains the refreshing realism of their paper!) We were, we regret, unaware of this Swedish study at the time of our 1970 paper's writing: it would certainly have deserved an acknowledgement at that time. However, we rather think the 'room' given by international prices is subsidiary to their model: the 8% to 9% wage increase could be attributed to high productivity growth in particular branches within the 'competitive sector'.

(3) Edgren, Faxén and Odhner, *loc. cit.* Table 1, p. 143.

(4) *ibid.* p. 149.

(5) *ibid.* p. 146.

(6) *ibid.* Table 1, p. 143.

continues. We might therefore also call this type of inflation, which is characteristic of so large a part of the world in the post-war era, 'equilibrium wage-productivity inflation'.

We reserve for future consideration various subsidiary implications of this analysis, such as those for income distribution, and for employment in the Third World.[1]

We would, however, make three comments on the foregoing analysis. First, on the concept of 'wage-leadership' which is involved in it. Here one must distinguish between the economic and social mechanisms which will tend to induce comparable pay-rates to follow the movement of wages in what were called above the 'key' industries, and the institutional processes by which formal pay-rates are adjusted. It is quite possible that pay in the key industries will be increased with very little friction in labour relations – perhaps, even, to a large extent by a 'wage drift' of incentive bonuses, payments (or 'fringes') made at managerial initiative, and so on. The critical struggles in the general movement of wages may then occur in quite other sectors of the negotiating system – perhaps in industries or public services where actual earnings have fallen behind relatively, perhaps at a quasi-political level (around a national minimum wage or central arbitration decision), so that industries other than the 'key' ones may *appear* as pattern-setters.

On the other hand, one must also suppose that there is a certain 'threshold effect' in the comparative perception of relative wage-movements. It is well known that small groups of workers (certain skilled specialists, for instance) have occasionally enjoyed preferential wage-increases over long periods without this leading to any general pressure for comparable advances from other employees. Even within the 'key' industries themselves, it is probable that – in the short run at least – there is generally some dispersal in rates of wage-increase between different groups of workers. It seems reasonable to suggest that the workers benefitting from wage increases which reflect a high productivity growth rate must reach a sufficient number, or a sufficient concentration, or be of an occupational character or organisation which permits fairly direct comparison with external groups, before their gain impacts on the perceptions of employers and workers in other industries.[2]

Secondly, while this analysis infers the average movements of wages, real wages, and retail prices to be determined by a system of relations to productivity growth, we do not suppose the causal connections to be altogether and exclusively one-way. Thus, it does not seem impossible that the wage-pressure which is transmitted from the 'key' industries to those where productivity growth is naturally (again, for either economic or technical reasons) low, may itself be a factor in inducing faster productivity growth

(1) For some reference to these, as for suggested resolutions to certain problems raised by the more detailed data there contained, see 'On the Determination of the General Wage Level, etc.', *loc. cit.*

(2) Such a 'threshold effect' would seem implicit in the analysis by Messrs. Eatwell, Llewellyn and Tarling, already referred to.

in the latter sectors — whether by capital-labour or (what might be called) management-labour substitution, by 'efficiency engineering' and so on.[1] So that, if it is true that the general growth of productivity has been faster in the past generation than it was previously, this may itself be to some extent a by-product of the predominant world inflation.

Thirdly (to quote the original paper) '... the model by no means denies the existence of other forces in wage and price determination: it merely traces in that process certain general, but apparently powerful, pressures whose detailed impact, and importance relative to other factors, may vary between economies'. Thus our Graph I suggests that within the long-run world inflationary trend there is still an international business cycle, which causes inflationary pressure to intensify and slacken by turns every few years.[2] And to movements of this kind such empirical observations as the Phillips Curve can be considered (as this monograph's *Introduction* perhaps indicates) relevant. Similarly, there are other pressures which may shift economies from the path of 'equilibrium' inflation temporarily — or even permanently: we shall discuss some such potential 'shocks' to the system later.

## Strato-inflation

The small group of economies in our Graph II which we categorise as 'strato-inflationary' is exotic. But their experience is important because of the further light it throws on the nature of recent inflation in general. About these economies, there are two questions to ask. The first involves the same problem we have already raised in relation to the majority group of countries which have experienced 'normal' or 'equilibrium' inflations: why should prices have tended to rise at just the rate they have? Half the countries in the strato-inflationary group have experienced rates very close to 30 per cent annually over the two decades the Graph covers, and the others are not far off: but this rate is ten times that of 'equilibrium' inflations. And the second question is: why the marked discontinuity between the two groups' experiences? No country, not the scene of a war, for which there exists a reasonably continuous record of average retail price movements over this period has had an annual inflation rate between 9.6 per cent and 21.6 per cent.

(1) This would be consistent with the results of our detailed study of post-war wage-movements in Holland (Turner and Jackson, 'On the Stability of Wage Differences and Productivity-based Wage Policies: An International Analysis', *British Journal of Industrial Relations*, March, 1969). Many cases could be cited from developing countries of wage-pressure leading directly to faster productivity growth despite a surplus of labour. A specific illustration is contained in an analysis of Turkish experience by D.A.S. Jackson (the results of which have been partially published in 'The Political Economy of Collective Bargaining — the case of Turkey', *British Journal of Industrial Relations*, March, 1971).

(2) Note that Graph I also includes economies of the 'strato-inflationary' type: both its average rate of inflation and its degree of fluctuation are thereby perceptibly increased.

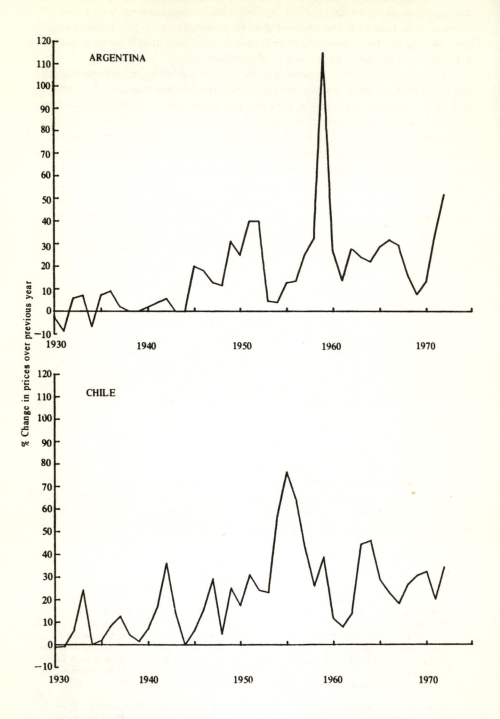

Graph III. Annual rate of inflation in two South American economies.

In fact, the discontinuity is in one sense even greater than it appears from Graph II. Only two of the 'industrialised market economies' in our histogram have had average rates of inflation above 6 per cent annually.[1] The small number of countries which have had rates between 6 and 10 per cent are all less developed economies — of which one or two might be said to be obviously trembling on the brink of strato-inflation. In another sense, however, the discontinuity is less than the histogram suggests. Apart from the Korean War year of 1951, it has been very unusual for price level fluctuations in any industrial economy to send its rate of inflation above 10 per cent in any twelvemonth. But in strato-inflationary countries, variations in the annual rate of national price increase are so wide that these have quite frequently brought it down to near that figure.

We illustrate this by our Graph III, which shows the yearly increase in prices for two of the more important of these economies since 1930. For the Argentine, at least, it is rather the considerable annual fluctuation in prices than any continued increase of them which is notable until the post-war period. And though it was popularly held in Chile that 1970 witnessed the turn of that country's first century of inflation, it is clear that this was not persistent before the 1940's. In the Chilean case, it was rather a previous history of intermittent inflationary bouts that prepared the way for the subsequent strato-inflation.

What also appears from Graph III is that, if the annual rate of inflation in these two countries has rarely fallen below 10 per cent in the years since World War II, it has also on only one occasion risen much above 50 per cent — an experience which was apparently sufficiently traumatic to deter any recurrence of the event. While it is difficult to generalise from such a small number of economies as those in the strato-inflationary group for which useful data is available, this fluctuation between a 10 per cent 'floor' and a 50 per cent 'ceiling' seems fairly typical of their recent experience; and if we can explain that phenomenon we should, of course, also explain their 30 per cent average rate.

A major clue is that these sharp fluctuations in the general rate of price increase have also been accompanied by marked changes in the distribution of income. For instance, from a United Nations Study, *Economic Development and Income Distribution in Argentina*, we take the following Table 4.

(1) By the same token, none of the industrial capitalist economies have had rates of less than 2 per cent. Non-communist countries below this figure have, moreover, mostly been moving up to the 'normal' rate over the period.

Table 4. *Percentage shares of total family income in Argentina*[1]

| Income Group: | 1953 | 1959 | 1961 |
|---|---|---|---|
| lowest 20% | 8 | 7 | 7 |
| Middle 50% (21—70) | 33 | 29 | 31 |
| Top 10% | 37 | 42 | 39 |

Here, the increased inequality in the distribution of income after 1953, with a shift towards the top 10 per cent of incomes away from others, and especially from the middle 50 per cent, was the result of policy changes, particularly in 1959 when 'stabilisation measures' resulted in a large transfer of income to profits. The distribution in 1953, however, was itself representative of the policy of the Peron era when the share of wage and salary income was substantially and deliberately increased.[2] On the other hand, Table 4 also shows that something of a reaction against the subsequent shift back to big property incomes set in again between 1959 and 1961. These transfers of income tend, therefore, to be rapidly reversed, and the switches are radically connected with the process of inflation itself.

The strato-inflationary sequence, however, can be studied most easily for Chile, whose long experience of it goes back to 1860, when the unregulated issue of paper currency by private banks was permitted and a considerable inflation followed, resulting in the suspension of currency convertibility in 1878.[3] This was the first of several such episodes, which were suggested by a very eminent economic historian of Latin America, the late David Joslin,[4] to be intimately connected with the fact that the dominant mining interests (nitrate, and later copper) benefitted from devaluation because they earned foreign currency but paid their wages and other charges in depreciated local money. Each of these episodes, however, led to the development of labour organisations aimed at protecting their members' real standards of living. Thus, one of the worst episodes was the inflation from 1904 to 1907 when Treasury note circulation trebled.[5] This had a considerable impact on the living standards of the growing urban workforce, and the resulting wave of industrial unrest culminated in the shooting of some 500 nitrate miners in 1907.[6] Such events stimulated the very early consolidation (for

(1) *Ibid.* (New York, 1969). Table 1, p. 3.

(2) *Ibid.* pp. 10 and 106.

(3) G. Subercaseaux *Monetary and Banking Policy in Chile* (Clarendon Press, Oxford, 1922) pp. 75, 85—93.

(4) In a discussion just before his death with one of the present writers; see D. Joslin, *A Century of Banking in Latin America* (Oxford University Press, London, 1963), pp. 188 ff., in which he identifies the landowners, too, as both benefitting from early devaluations and being the strongest political force.

(5) Subercaseaux, op. cit. p. 200: the total circulation of treasury notes rose from 50 million pesos to 150 million pesos.

(6) R.J. Alexander, *Organised Labor in Latin America* (Free Press, New York, 1965), p. 86.

a developing country) of trade unionism and a labour movement in Chile —
an event which was itself an important background to that country's acquisi-
tion of a Marxist government by election in 1970. The Gran Federacion
Obrera de Chile was founded in 1909, and thereafter strikes and inflation
became inseparable phenomena, both in practical affairs and in theoretical
discussions.[1]

The worst crises of Chilean society occurred at times when rising prices
coincided with stagnant or falling production. Chile was very badly hit by
the Depression, both economically and politically; and in mid-1932 one of
the transient governments of the period started a programme of public
works financed by borrowing. The money supply and the price index doubled
within a few *months*; and the accompanying labour unrest led to the formation and eventual election of the radical Popular Front, which 'marks the
beginning of the modern phase of Chile's inflation'.[2] It is significant of
that government's predominant social character, however, that it began to
decree general percentage *salary* increases to compensate for increases in
the cost of living: manual workers pressed for similar arrangements, and in
time these adjustments became both general and automatic, which led to a
recurrent escalation of wage-price inflation. Similar 'indexisation' devices
were incorporated into farm price controls (or supports), and into controls
over industrial and other charges, so that the escalation was accentuated.
From the development of this structure of group-defensive institutional
arrangements, the economy oscillated between escalating inflation and
attempts at deflation — which in turn induced resistance from those groups
which suffered from them.

By the 1940's the lines of social division in Chile were thus sharply
drawn; while the (largely foreign-owned) mining companies, and the landowners and business communities were recognisable as distinct group
interests, even between the well-educated middle class and the working
class there was a very considerable ideological and political gap. On the
one hand this led to Congressional refusals to implement desirable economic
and social reforms, and on the other to trade union refusals to cooperate
against inflation by moderating wage demands. As industrial solutions to the
problems of wage-price determination were not available, both sides had to
seek the mediation of the government.[3] But this also meant that the only
beneficiaries of government policies have been organised groups: the desperate
'marginalistas' (the urban unemployed, the landless peasantry, the unorganised and often homeless casual labourers) tended to get nothing.[4]

(1) F.W. Fetter, *Monetary Inflation in Chile* (Princeton University Press, 1931)
     makes this comment on p. 122.

(2) A. Hirschman, *Journeys towards Progress* (Twentieth Century Fund, 1963),
     ch. 3, tells the story in detail.

(3) The results of the process are clearly traced by J. Petras in *Political and
     Social Forces in Chilean Development* (University of California, 1969).

(4) See K. Griffin: 'Reflections on Latin American Development', *Oxford Economic
     Papers*, March, 1966, or 'Take-off for the top 10%: the social implications of
     Brazil's development', Kevin Rafferty, *Financial Times*, 1 August 1972, p. 5.

It could be held that the successive peaks of Chilean inflation have risen basically because, while particular groups (landowners, export industries, businessmen or employees) could engineer an expansion of currency, credit or public spending in their interest, other groups could prevent the government raising taxation to cover the cost. But these groups could not prevent their members meeting the cost another way, by higher prices, and this led to a system of group-defensive organisation which was also mutually retaliatory. Thus a wage-fixing process developed by which the government decreed annually an increase in minimum wages (and salaries) equivalent to the previous year's rise in living costs. On this base, the more powerful unions would proceed to bargain for additional increases to cover increased productivity, plus some part of the anticipated future rise in prices. Farm prices were guaranteed so as to protect farmers' real income against the consequent rise in industrial prices, and industrial prices were fixed (often by legal controls) to cover the anticipated increases in wages and raw material charges and to protect profits in real terms.

The system inherently involved – granted its initial instability and the large monetary increases that were required to protect the position of individual groups – a cumulative inflation. And this in turn provoked periodic attempts at 'stabilisation', by severe deflations, credit squeezes, wage freezes and the like – for instance, in 1950, 1954, and 1956. But these in turn induced violent social conflict – there was a general strike in 1954. And every such attempt at stabilisation was finally defeated because the reaction of particular groups to the measures of control or deflation involved was so violent that the government abandoned the effort (the attempt by President Frei, the last government before the present Allende administration, to halt inflation was finally defeated by the unions' refusal to accept a further tapering-off of wage-increases, and by subsequent strikes).

The process of strato-inflation is thus essentially one in which, *past* inflation having proceeded to the point at which major deprivation has been experienced by particular social groups, these then organise, not merely for their future protection, but to recover lost ground. Retaliatory-defensive mechanisms are then built up by other groups, so that the inflation accelerates. However, the process is not unlimited, because there comes a point at which the rate of price inflation is so high that the institutional mechanisms involved can no longer function adequately – partly because of the time they take (major legislative regulations or industrial negotiations can hardly take place more often than annually), partly because it becomes quite impossible to predict what prices will be within the term of the settlement, or even to establish what the current price level actually is: 'index-watching' and acrimonious dispute over the meaning and accuracy of the monthly price-indices are obsessional pre-occupations in these economies. At a really high rate of inflation, the *monthly* deterioration in real income to those whose pay or revenue is, even in the short term, fixed, becomes very perceptible (see Table 5).

Table 5. *Percentage rate of price inflation: alternative perceptions*

| Annually | — equals — | Monthly |
|:---:|:---:|:---:|
| 6 | | 0.5 |
| 10 | | 0.8 |
| 13 | | 1 |
| 20 | | 1½ |
| 27 | | 2 |
| 35 | | 2½ |
| 42 | | 3 |
| 51 | | 3½ |
| 60 | | 4 |
| 80 | | 5 |
| 100 | | 6 |

Industrial and social conflict increases, there are demonstrations against the authorities, even spontaneous 'unofficial', 'unconstitutional' or illegal strikes as workers attempt to obtain 'interim' pay increases to maintain their standards of living, and so on.

When the rate of inflation approaches 3 or 4 per cent a month, fear of a collapse of the institutional-protective mechanisms and of group living standards becomes so intense, that demands develop for drastic government action. And the disparate social groups are temporarily prepared to support, or at least to acquiesce in, very severe measures to halt the spiral and bring the rate of price increase under control. The tendency for a 'panic' mentality to develop as inflation nears the 50 per cent annual rate is fairly well recognised in strato-inflationary countries.[1] However, once the immediate crisis is over, there will still be many groups which feel that they have lost out in the preceding sequence, and will wish to recover their lost ground. Other groups will feel specifically disadvantaged by the measures taken to halt the spiral. And in general, after any substantial experience of strato-inflation, there is a limit to organised groups' credence in the capacity of governments to halt the process, and thus to the minimum increase in money income that they will accept as reasonably insuring them against irrecoverable future loss.

An illustration of the difficulty — if not impossibility — of holding the annual rate of inflation below 10 per cent in such a context is conveyed by Argentinian experience since the mid-60's (see Table 6). Price inflation during 1965 had been severe, and the Illia government attempted to reduce it by decreeing a maximum for wage increases of 15 per cent. But employees and businessmen continued to compensate themselves

---

(1) We base this observation on extensive discussions with economists, bankers, financial officials and union leaders in Santiago, as well as other Latin American capitals, in 1970. But see also (for instance) Dr Roberto Campos: 'Inflations in Latin America usually began to be combated after they had reached a rate of 50 per cent per annum. Prior to that point, they were apt not to be taken seriously'. (in *Economic Development for Latin America* edited by H.S. Ellis, London, Macmillan, 1961, p. 27) — an opinion also cited approvingly by the late David Joslin, *op. cit.*

Table 6. *Monthly rate of price inflation in Argentina, 1966*

| | |
|---|---|
| Jan./Feb. | 2.5 |
| Feb./March | 2.6 |
| March/April | 1.3 |
| April/May | 2.6 |
| May/June | 5.5 |
| June/July | 0.1 |

for previous increases in costs, and as inflation continued the policy of
wage restraint came increasingly under attack through widespread strikes.
In May food prices alone rose by 7.7 per cent; and so there was an air of
public relief when the military intervened, deposing the civilian government
and issuing a proclamation condemning 'the state of anarchy resulting in an
antagonistic alignment of forces, which was the more serious in that elemen-
tary social considerations were completely ignored.' The proclamation went
on to promise not only to restore social discipline but also to eliminate
inflation, described as 'the most terrible scourge by which any society can
be afflicted, especially the low-income sectors'.

The new government, however, did not conceive that the ensuing battle
against inflation could begin until the power of the trade unions had been
greatly reduced. Towards the end of the year it successfully suspended the
port workers' union, and broke a strike of dockers against rationalisation.
In March, 1967, most of the powerful unions were suspended and their bank
accounts blocked when they participated in a one-day strike that had been
declared illegal.

Following this 'conquest' the way was open for a wage policy based on
a general wage adjustment intended to bring everyone to approximately the
same 'historical' relative position, followed by a wage freeze. Price control
was also introduced, together with (the Krieger Vasena Program) increased
taxation, reduced government expenditure, and a national investment plan.
But the wage control was more effective than the price control, and in 1968
there was a sharp fall in real earnings (see Table 7).

The fall in real wages bore most heavily upon the low paid workers,
particularly the non-unionised groups. Although the economy had been
skilfully reflated and a state of near full employment was reached, the
acquiescence essential for the success of the stabilisation policy disa-
ppeared as income distribution moved against the workers. Organised and
unorganised demands for wage increases built up during 1968, even though
the rate of price inflation was falling quickly. The critical point came when
the government attempted to compensate higher-paid employees for reductions
in pay-differentials induced by previous wage-inflation. In May 1969 there
were violent riots in Cordoba and other provincial towns and the trade
unions once more began a series of one-day general strikes.

In October the Argentinian government abandoned its wage policy,
decreeing a flat rate general wage increase of 3,000 pesos a month with
promises of more to come. The 'emergency' wage increase was deliberately
designed to appease the lower income groups, but as more and more was
conceded by the government, prices began to rise and inflation once again

Table 7. *Wage and price movements in Argentina*

| Percentage change over previous year | 1966 | 1967 | 1968 | 1969 | 1970* |
|---|---|---|---|---|---|
| Negotiated money wages | 34 | 30 | 5 | 7 | 14 |
| Prices | 32 | 25 | 17 | 8 | 15 |
| Real wage rates | 2 | 4 | −10 | −1 | −1 |

\* First seven months

accelerated. It had proven impracticable, despite the partial suppression of unions and a most carefully-conceived and comprehensive programme of economic and fiscal regulation and of income manipulation, to hold the rate of inflation below 10 per cent in the face of the mistrust and sense of relative deprivation of major social groups.

Thus we can see that even a determined and successful stabilisation programme in a politically 'favourable' environment depends upon an at least implicit socio-political consensus, and will break down when this fails. People may continue to demand a minimum rate of monetary wage or income increase as an insurance against the failure of the policy, or against discrimination in income distribution. Even if they are promised a zero rate of price inflation by the programme, prudence dictates insistence on a minimum income increase as a reasonable cover. In the strato-inflationary economies, and for wages, this increase tends to be one of at least the standard deviation of past rates of price inflation − i.e. of past experience, which is about 10 per cent.

The upper and low boundaries of 'strato-inflation' are thus determined largely by psycho-social reactions to, and a consequent 'feedback' effect upon, the going rate of general price increase. And the *lower* boundary of strato-inflation tends also to be, as we have shown, the *upper* boundary of 'normal' or 'equilibrium' inflations, which is thus determined in the same way. In either group, an approach to the upper boundary is signalled or accompanied by an intensification of industrial and social conflict, which itself commonly provides the main pressure on governments to organise a retreat from this dangerous frontier. (We show in this Paper's second study how the accelerated inflation of 1968 onwards induced a major wave of industrial unrest in Britain: and it was the near-10 per cent rate of price increase there in 1970−71 that compelled Mr. Heath's new government to withdraw from its initial hostility to 'incomes and prices policies' and make the first moves towards a revived Conservative version of one).

In the strato-inflationary economies, however, the general level of social conflict is in any case notably higher than in the countries of the 'equilibrium' inflation band. (The incidence of *recorded* strikes in Chile in the 1960's was ten times higher than that in Britain − for an approximately ten times faster rate of general price increase). And this introduces a major difference between the two types of inflation. In the equilibrium-inflationary economies, social and industrial conflict is mostly about the distribution of the yearly (marginal) additions to the national product: the basic distribution of income, whether between social classes or economic groups remains relatively stable from year to year. But in the strato-inflations, social conflict centres on the basic distribution of income itself.

Thus, when retail prices are rising at 3 or 4 per cent annually, the short-term depreciation of real living standards, even for groups whose incomes are absolutely fixed in between institutional adjustments, is (as Table 5 shows) barely significant. And for most people, there are various compensatory and semi-automatic mechanisms which at least partially offset rising prices. White-collar employees commonly have annual seniority increments, many manual workers benefit from one form or another of 'wage drift' (like incentive bonuses or piece-rate payments affected by rising production), individuals in both classes gain by promotion at work or from the gradual movement of labour to higher-paying jobs, and so on. It is only in periods when the rate of inflation accelerates temporarily that large sections of the population suffer perceptible short-term loss in real income.

Under strato-inflation, however, the situation is quite otherwise. When prices are rising at 30 per cent a year, and the processes of income determination become (a normal accompaniment to this situation) highly institutionalised — if not absolutely politicised — almost every major social group will inevitably experience severe short-term depreciation of real living standards. This can be shown by Graph IV, which supposes a general yearly wage-adjustment in a situation when *real* wages are increasing 3 per cent a year on average and in the long run.

Immediately after the wage-increase, workers' real income will be 15 per cent above trend. But it will fall 30 per cent in the year's course, and be 15

Graph IV. Real wages under strato-inflation.

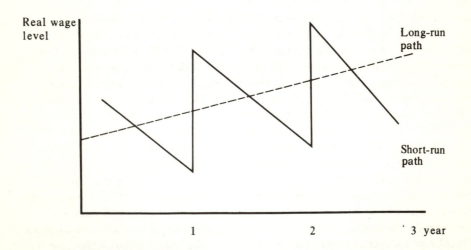

per cent *below* trend just before the next round of wage-adjustments.[1] From which three things follow. First, that almost everybody can sincerely feel that *his* real income is falling when *average* real incomes are rising. Secondly, since *all* income increases are not synchronised,[2] the groups which are, at any given moment, most severely afflicted by a sense of deprivation will also inevitably feel that their loss has been someone else's gain. And thirdly, that any one group's target standard of a 'just' real income – i.e. that to which it feels reasonably entitled by past experience of what is possible – will be related to that which it in fact experienced just after its last income increase. But since this standard is 15 per cent above trend, it is inevitable that the demands of all organised groups together will exceed the immediately realisable (or foreseeable) capacity of the economy.

Which returns us to our initial point, that a struggle over income distribution, and the instability of income distribution which it both engenders and springs from, is the mechanism central to this variety of inflation.

## Inflation and world trade: the international regulators

There is, however, one other major difference between the 'equilibrium' and the 'strato'-inflations. This is a difference in the respective relationship of price movements within the individual countries concerned to those in the world as a whole. And since these relationships also appear as another important determinant of the pace of specific national inflations, they are perhaps worth looking at in some detail.

It has been noted elsewhere that in every European country the prices of exported goods and services have risen by less than the average price increase for total final expenditure.[3] The study concerned adduced two reasons for this: one, that a large proportion of European exports were manufactures, the price of which had risen less than those of other commodities; and two, that the indices were current weighted, so reflecting shifts towards items whose price had risen relatively less. But it was also

---

(1) In such situations the increases in wages are far greater than increases in productivity, of course; these cost savings being now a merely minor change. Thus, we could continue our formalisation of p. 26, n. 1, as follows, for this type of inflation (where $b$, $c$ and $d$ are parameters):

$$\left(\frac{\Delta w}{w}\right)_t = c + b\left(\frac{\Delta p}{p}\right)_{t-1} \quad \text{where } b > 1 \tag{6}$$

and

$$\left(\frac{\Delta p}{p}\right)_t = d\left(\frac{\Delta w}{w}\right)_t \quad \text{where } d \geq 1 \tag{7}$$

so that

$$\left(\frac{\Delta p}{p}\right)_t = cd + bd\left(\frac{\Delta p}{p}\right)_{t-1} \quad \text{where } bd > 1 \tag{8}$$

(2) Otherwise the process could hardly continue. This is why a synchronisation of income increases is a necessary first step (but only a first step) to the reduction of strato-inflation.

(3) United Nations, *Incomes in Post-War Europe* (Economic Commission for Europe, Geneva, 1967), Chapter 2.

Table 8 *International connections between*

| | Australia | Belgium | Canada | Denmark | Finland | France | Iceland | Ireland | Italy | Luxembourg | Netherlands | New Zealand | Norway | Sweden | U.K. | U.S.A. | Argentina | Barbados | Bolivia | Brazil | British Honduras | Chile | Colombia | Puerto Rico |
|---|---|---|---|---|---|---|---|---|---|---|---|---|---|---|---|---|---|---|---|---|---|---|---|---|
| Australia | 10 | 6 | | 6 | 7 | 5 | 5 | | 6 | | 7 | 7 | 7 | 8 | 5 | | | 8 | | | 7 | −5 | | |
| Belgium | | 10 | 6 | 6 | 5 | | 6 | 5 | 7 | | 5 | 5 | 7 | 7 | 5 | 8 | | | | | 6 | | | 8 |
| Canada | | | 10 | 6 | 8 | 6 | 6 | | 9 | | 8 | 6 | 7 | 7 | 5 | 8 | | 6 | | | 7 | | | |
| Denmark | | | | 10 | 7 | | 5 | | 5 | | 5 | | 5 | 5 | 6 | | | 4 | | | 6 | | | |
| Finland | | | | | 10 | 6 | 7 | | 7 | | 8 | 5 | 6 | 5 | 5 | 5 | 7 | | | | 5 | | | |
| France | | | | | | 10 | | | | | 6 | 4 | 5 | 5 | 5 | | | 5 | | | 5 | −4 | | |
| Iceland | | | | | | | 10 | 5 | 5 | 5 | 6 | 5 | 7 | 6 | 6 | 6 | 6 | | | | 7 | | | |
| Ireland | | | | | | | | 10 | 6 | | 5 | 7 | 6 | 8 | 6 | | | 7 | | | 5 | | | 6 |
| Italy | | | | | | | | | 10 | | 4 | 7 | 7 | 5 | 5 | | | | | | 5 | | | 6 |
| Luxembourg | | | | | | | | | | 10 | 9 | | | 5 | 5 | | | | | | 5 | | | |
| Netherlands | | | | | | | | | | | 10 | | | 5 | | | | | | | 5 | | | |
| New Zealand | | | | | | | | | | | | 10 | 9 | 6 | 7 | 6 | | 7 | | | 8 | | | 6 |
| Norway | | | | | | | | | | | | | 10 | 8 | 8 | 8 | | 7 | | | 9 | | | 7 |
| Sweden | | | | | | | | | | | | | | 10 | 8 | 8 | | 7 | | | 9 | | | 6 |
| U.K. | | | | | | | | | | | | | | | 10 | 6 | | 8 | | | 8 | | | 5 |
| U.S.A. | | | | | | | | | | | | | | | | 10 | | 6 | | | 7 | | | 8 |
| Argentina | | | | | | | | | | | | | | | | | 10 | | | | | | | |
| Barbados | | | | | | | | | | | | | | | | | | 10 | | | 9 | | | 6 |
| Bolivia | | | | | | | | | | | | | | | | | | | 10 | | | | 5 | |
| Brazil | | | | | | | | | | | | | | | | | | | | 10 | | | | |
| British Honduras | | | | | | | | | | | | | | | | | | | | | 10 | | | 6 |
| Chile | | | | | | | | | | | | | | | | | | | | | | 10 | | |
| Colombia | | | | | | | | | | | | | | | | | | | | | | | 10 | |
| Puerto Rico | | | | | | | | | | | | | | | | | | | | | | | | 10 |

Correlation coefficients
between annual rates of change in
pairs of national retail price indices.
These coefficients have been rounded off
to one decimal place and multiplied by ten:
e.g., so that − 0.447 becomes − 4 ('out of 10').
All correlations are significant at the 5% level
(two tail test).

| Country | Salvador | Cambodia | Hong Kong | Iran | Malaysia | Pakistan | Thailand | Camerouns | Congo-B'ville | Egypt | Kenya | Madagascar | Mauritius | Morocco | Mozambique | South Africa | Rhodesia | Tanzania | Tunisia | Uganda | Cyprus | Malta | Portugal | Turkey |
|---|---|---|---|---|---|---|---|---|---|---|---|---|---|---|---|---|---|---|---|---|---|---|---|---|
| Australia | 5 | 5 | 7 | | 5 | 5 | 5 | | | | 7 | 6 | 8 | 6 | 9 | 8 | 8 | 6 | | | 5 | 7 | -5 | |
| Belgium | | 6 | | | | | | | | 6 | | | | | | | | | | | 6 | 5 | | |
| Canada | | | 6 | 9 | | | | | 5 | 6 | | 7 | | | 5 | 6 | | 5 | | | 5 | 5 | | |
| Denmark | | | 6 | | | | | | | 5 | | 5 | | | | | | | | | | | | |
| Finland | 5 | 5 | 8 | | | | | | | 5 | | 5 | | | | 5 | | | | | 5 | 5 | | |
| France | 5 | 5 | 6 | | | 8 | 8 | | | | 7 | 6 | 7 | | 5 | 8 | | 6 | | | | | | |
| Iceland | 5 | -5 | 7 | | | | | | | 5 | | 6 | | | | 5 | | | | | | 6 | | -6 |
| Ireland | | | | | 4 | 8 | | | | | | 6 | | | | 6 | | 6 | | | 4 | | | |
| Italy | | | | | 5 | | | | | | | | | | | | | | | | | | | |
| Luxembourg | | | 6 | | 8 | | | | 5 | 7 | 6 | 5 | 5 | 5 | | 5 | | | 6 | | | | | |
| Netherlands | 6 | 6 | 8 | | | | | | 4 | 6 | | | | | | | | | | | | | | |
| New Zealand | 6 | | 6 | 6 | | | | | | 5 | | 7 | | | 7 | 5 | 7 | | | | 6 | 6 | | |
| Norway | 5 | | 8 | 6 | | | | | | 5 | | 7 | | | 7 | 5 | 6 | | | | 7 | 7 | | |
| Sweden | | | 8 | 6 | | | | | 5 | 5 | | 7 | | | 6 | | | | | | 6 | 6 | | |
| U.K. | | | 6 | 7 | | | | | | 6 | | 7 | | | 8 | 5 | 8 | 5 | | | 6 | 5 | | |
| U.S.A. | | | 8 | 5 | | | | | | 6 | | | | | | 5 | | | | | 7 | 6 | | |
| Argentina | | | 5 | | | | | | | | | | | | | | | | | | | | | 6 |
| Barbados | | | 6 | | 7 | | | | | 6 | | 9 | | | 5 | 8 | 6 | 7 | | | 5 | 7 | | |
| Bolivia | | | | | | | | | | | | | | | | | | | | | | | | |
| Brazil | -5 | | | | | | | | | -4 | | -5 | | | | -5 | | | | | | | | |
| British Honduras | | | 7 | | 6 | | | | 5 | 6 | | 7 | | | 7 | 6 | 6 | | | | 6 | 8 | | |
| Chile | | | | | | | | | | | | -5 | | | | -4 | | | | | | | | |
| Colombia | | | | | | | | | | | | | | | | | | | | | | | | |
| Puerto Rico | | | | | 5 | 6 | | | | | | | | | | | | | | | 6 | 6 | | |
| Salvador | 10 | 5 | 6 | | | | | | | 5 | | | | | | | | | | | 5 | | -6 | -5 |
| Cambodia | | 10 | | | | | | | | | | | -5 | | | | | | | | | | | -5 |
| Hong Kong | | | 10 | | 5 | | 5 | 7 | | | 6 | 5 | | | | | | 5 | | | | | | |
| Iran | | | | 10 | | | | | | | | | | | | | | | | | | | | 5 |
| Malaysia | | | | | 10 | | | | 5 | 5 | | 6 | | | 6 | 5 | 5 | | | | 6 | 6 | | |
| Pakistan | | | | | | 10 | | | | | | | | | | | | | | | | | | |
| Thailand | | | | | | | 10 | | | 7 | | 5 | | | 7 | | | 7 | | | 7 | 4 | | |
| Camerouns | | | | | | | | 10 | 9 | | | 9 | 8 | | 5 | 7 | | | 8 | | | | | |
| Congo-B'ville | | | | | | | | | 10 | | | 9 | 8 | | | 6 | | | 8 | | | | | |
| Egypt | | | | | | | | | | 10 | | | | | | | | | | | | | | |
| Kenya | | | | | | | | | | | 10 | | | | 7 | 5 | 7 | | | | 5 | 5 | -6 | |
| Madagascar | | | | | | | | | | | | 10 | 8 | | 6 | 7 | | 9 | | | | | | |
| Mauritius | | | | | | | | | | | | | 10 | | 8 | 6 | 7 | | | | | 6 | | -5 |
| Morocco | | | | | | | | | | | | | | 10 | | 5 | 6 | | 9 | | | | | |
| Mozambique | | | | | | | | | | | | | | | 10 | | | | | | | | | |
| South Africa | | | | | | | | | | | | | | | | 10 | 7 | 9 | 6 | | 5 | | | |
| Rhodesia | | | | | | | | | | | | | | | | | 10 | 5 | 6 | | 5 | | | |
| Tanzania | | | | | | | | | | | | | | | | | | 10 | | | 5 | | | |
| Tunisia | | | | | | | | | | | | | | | | | | | 10 | | | | | |
| Uganda | | | | | | | | | | | | | | | | | | | | 10 | | | | |
| Cyprus | | | | | | | | | | | | | | | | | | | | | 10 | 6 | -5 | |
| Malta | | | | | | | | | | | | | | | | | | | | | | 10 | | |
| Portugal | | | | | | | | | | | | | | | | | | | | | | | 10 | |
| Turkey | | | | | | | | | | | | | | | | | | | | | | | | 10 |

41

observed that the prices of exported manufactures had risen less than domestic industrial prices. The study did not go beyond this, but the implication is clearly that international trading prices are an important restraining factor in national inflations.[1] The other side of the coin, however, is that common international inflation may give particular countries more 'room' to raise domestic monetary incomes, and thus also prices.[2] So that national price-levels could be expected to move in concert to some degree: and that this is indeed empirically the case, our Table 1 (p. 19) offers some evidence.

Thus, Graph I showed, as well as we were able to trace it, the course of world inflation (or rather, since that is a nebulous concept, the average of all adequately recorded national inflations in the non-communist world) from 1948. Comparing that with the average rates of inflation for *groups* of countries by 5-year periods, the effect of the Korean boom is almost everywhere apparent: in only two of the six groups distinguished by Table 1 was the average rate of increase in prices not markedly higher in 1948/53 than in the succeeding five years. Similarly in all groups the average rate of inflation was unusually low in the period 1958/63 (mainly because of the general recession in which the 1950's terminated, and which produced an abnormally low rate of world price increase in from 1959 to 1962).

There are two ways in which we can study these international linkages of inflation more closely: by considering the relations between price movements in individual countries, and by examining (again) the connections within and between groups of economies in more detail. As a basis for this we have compiled the matrix of which our Table 8 presents a selected and summary picture. In this matrix annual price-movements since 1948, for each non-communist country for which this data was available at the time the matrix was compiled, were compared with those of every other country (subject to similar limitations), and a calculation was made of the extent to which price-trends in every pair of countries were significantly correlated — that is, of whether changes in prices in each pair moved around their averages in the same direction at the same time.[3] Thus, reading across the first row of the summary Table, it will be seen that price-movements in Australia showed a significant positive correlation of 0.6 and 0.7 with those in

(1) A point developed in Hicks' Essay 7, *Essays in World Economics, op. cit.*

(2) As shown by Edgren, Faxén and Odhner, *loc. cit.*, for the Swedish case.

(3) Because of non-availability of sufficient more recent data at the time when the matrix was constructed, it covers the period 1948—1968, and only 74 countries (against the 81 of Graph I). This gives, nevertheless, 2,701 pairs of observations, of which nearly one-third showed significant correlations. In this case, moreover, the usual difficulty with differences in national price indices' construction, which would in any case produce merely statistical variations between national average price-movements and thus obscure the degree of real correlation, is compounded by such facts as: e.g., some indices consisting predominantly of food, others of manufactures, commodity groups the average prices of which we have occasionally moved in different directions.

Canada and France respectively, no significant correlation with those in Belgium or Denmark, and so on. Similarly, reading down the Table's last *column,* Turkish price-trends are found to have few correlations with those in other countries; and in the cases where a significant linkage is found, several are *negative,* as with Iceland and Mauritius — meaning that prices in Turkey have (granted the general inflationary trend) increased little at times when those in Iceland and Mauritius were rising fast and *vice versa).*

The Table can thus be read in two dimensions: on the one hand we can take the *intensity* of linkage between price-movements in particular pairs of countries (so as to say, for instance, that the average coefficient of linkage between Australian retail price-movements and those in *all* other countries for which data existed was 0.349, while that for Turkey was *minus* 0.168.[1] But in general, countries which show high coefficients in price-movements relative to other countries also show a larger number of significant linkages, so it is easier to consider instead the proportion of these which any country exhibits.

Thus it is immediately clear that the industrialised countries show a much more frequent linkage of price-movements among themselves than do the less developed economies. If we consider the industrial 'market' economies as a group, for instance, and compare their internal price linkage with that within regional groups of developing countries, we get the picture shown by Table 9.[2]

The very high degree of linkage in price-movements between the industrial capitalist economies is clearly in part a reflection of the extent to which they now trade with each other (rather than with economies of other kinds), and in part a consequence of competition between them in the world trade in manufactures. Countries which show a high correlation (over 80 per cent) with other countries within the group include Scandinavia and U.S.A., a position which makes self-evident sense; the U.K. is about average here (but also shows an unusually large number of correlations with prices in developing countries). It is notable that the three industrialised countries which have — for different reasons — enjoyed a very strong balance of payments position over the past generation, Japan, West Germany and Switzerland, display a low degree of correlation with other countries, either in the industrial group or in the world as a whole (the Japanese percentage is below 15 in either category). Thus the very strong trade advantage of these

(1) In these two calculations, correlations which proved non-significant on test are counted as zero — i.e. the sum of all significant correlations of country pairs (34 such for Australia) is divided by the number of possible pairs. Similarly, significant negative correlations (5 for Turkey) are summed to offset significant positive correlations. The Australian positive score is thus very high: moreover, the existence of negative correlations between pairs of economies implies that it would in any case be impossible for any country to show significant positive correlations with *all* others.

(2) This excludes six Mediterranean countries, where only 4 correlations between pairs are significant, but of these, 3 (for Portugal) are negative.

Table 9. *International linkages in price inflation*

(Number within each group of significantly correlated pairs of national
retail price-indices as a proportion of all possible distinct pairs)

| Economies | % of correlation |
|---|---|
| Industrialised Market (19) | 63 |
| African (17) | 28 |
| Asian (12) | 11 |
| Latin American and Caribbean (20) | 14 |
| Latin American etc. excluding strato-inflationary countries[a] (14) | 18 |

([a] As in Table I's alternative figure.)

three countries has to some extent insulated them against the effect of external price-movements.[1] Which is a further indicator of the importance of
those movements as regulating inflation in *other* countries.

The low percentage of price linkage between less developed countries is
mainly an index of the comparative weakness of merely regional pressures:
it is notable that even the separation of the strato-inflationary economies as
a separate group does not much raise the low degree of price-correlation
between Latin American countries.

However, although the less developed countries are not closely linked
amongst themselves, the position is quite otherwise when one considers
the connection of their price-movements with the average rate of inflation in
the industrialised countries. Thus the average rate of retail price increase
for our seventeen African countries is correlated annually with the average rate
of inflation in the industrial market economies at 69 per cent;[2] the average

(1) Obviously so in the case of Japan, which has been very much on the upper edge
of the 'normally' inflationary band over the whole period. For a note on the
peculiarities of wage determination in Japan, see the O.E.C.D., *Economic
Surveys: Japan* June 1971 (Paris, 1971), ch. 2 and Annex. The connection with
relatively low inflation rates in Germany and Switzerland (and mainly in the
1950's) is not so obvious, but can be argued to be at least a dual one.

(2) The equation for African prices with those in industrial market economies is:

$$\begin{bmatrix} \text{Average annual} \\ \text{price changes in} \\ \text{African countries} \end{bmatrix} = 0.49 + 0.997 \begin{bmatrix} \text{Average annual} \\ \text{price changes in} \\ \text{industrial economies} \end{bmatrix}$$

$$R^2 = 0.47$$

which shows an almost one-for-one linkage between the respective average
annual rates of inflation. The $R^2$ is not very high, but the model takes no
account of lags — of which there is a strong suggestion in the actual series.
Specific case studies of the effects of international raw-material price movements on internal cost inflation in developing countries are available from
J.B. Knight 'Wages and Zambia's Economic Development', in *Constraints on
the Economic Development of Zambia,* edited by C. Elliott (Oxford University
Press, 1971) and in two reports for the I.L.O. by one of the present writers on
incomes and prices problems and policy in Tanzania and Zambia: H.A. Turner,
*Report to the Government of the United Republic of Tanzania on Wages, Incomes
and Prices Policy* (Government Printer, Dar es Salaam, 1967) and *Report to
the Government of Zambia on Incomes, Wages and Prices in Zambia: Policy
and Machinery* (Government Printer, Lusaka, 1969).

for the twelve Asian countries correlates at 58 per cent; and the average for the fourteen 'equilibrium'-inflationary Latin American countries correlates with the industrial countries' overall index at 81 per cent. Obviously these connections reflect the 'client' situation of many less developed countries as suppliers of raw materials and importers of manufactures. And there are indeed individual examples of such a 'client' association: thus the correlation coefficient of the Puerto Rican with the United States price changes is 0.75, and that of the Tanzanian with the British is 0.76. One can note also that the developing countries with a high score of external price correlations are all ones that are smaller (and thus presumably in general more dependent). While the large developing economies, which are also in general more complex – India, Pakistan, Mexico, Brazil – have rather low scores.

The fact that the less developed economies on the average, however, show a lower degree of external price linkage than do industrial ones is presumably a factor which permits even those which may be classed as in our major group of 'normal' or 'equilibrium' inflations to vary rather more widely around that system's norm than do the industrial countries.[1] But what we must particularly note here is the position of the 'strato-inflationary' economies.

It is fairly evident from Table 8 that countries with a very low score of positive connections between domestic and external price-movements often show several significant *negative* connections: consider, for instance, Portugal, Iran and Turkey again. And the specific countries involved in such negative connections make no particular sense in trading terms. Thus the two countries with the highest score of negative external correlates are Portugal and Brazil: but there is not much overlap in the countries they have negative connections with, nor any dominating trade association between these two economies themselves. Their only obvious common factor is their language, and there is little other evidence that Portugese pre-disposes its speakers to behave contrarily.

In some cases, these negative external connections probably reflect an internal impact of world price movements which is delayed by local factors or autarchic regimes. (Thus Portugal in fact shows a rather similar pattern of external price-correlates to Spain, which is not included in Table 8). There has been – as Graph I perhaps suggests – a fairly distinct cyclical movement around the 'normal' inflationary trend in most countries, with peaks

---

(1) This would also provide a supporting explanation of the phenomenon we noted in the paper referred to earlier ('On the Determination of the General Wage Level, etc.'), that although *internal* rates of wage-increase vary more widely than within industrial economies, the LDC's average rate of inflation was the same (*ibid.* pp. 841/2). Weak external restraints may in some countries permit wages to rise faster than productivity growth even in the 'key' industries of our model. The effect of international price competition remains – as is evidenced by the LDC's average rate of inflation – but as a weakened force permitting also greater national variation.

(or troughs) occurring about every four years in the industrial economies, and these appear on the average to be reflected with a lag of a year or thereabouts in the less developed economies of Africa and Asia.[1] So that any further delay in an economy's reflection of these movements would show an inversion of external variations in the general rate of inflation. And since the particular countries with which this inversion happens to achieve numerical significance are clearly selected largely by statistical accident, this is another demonstration that national rates of inflation in general are a product of the combined effect of internal, national forces and of world restraints: regional circumstances and specific national trading connections remain, on the whole, rather subsidiary.

But in the economies of the strato-inflationary group we have a quite different position. Thus if we take the six South American countries listed in the note to our Table 1, we find that they all have a very low degree of correlation between their price movements and the external world — so that, if we were to adopt the index devised in passing for Australia and Turkey, above (p. 43) their average coefficient of external price-linkage would be only 0.016: a very low figure indeed.[2]

In effect the strato-inflationary countries have largely escaped from the regulators on internal price-movements which are imposed by external trade. But this they have done by repeated devaluations, which their governments used as a device to evade the dilemma between unpopularity caused by the economic and social effects of inflation and the unpopularity of deflation or controls. But (as our model of wage-price disequilibrium inflation shows) the consequent rise in internal prices has had secondary effects — particularly on the distribution of income — which are not now controllable. These Latin American countries have adopted continuous devaluation, but now cannot get back to the equilibrium rate of inflation because of the social conflicts and compensatory mechanisms which have built up in the disequilibrium situation. So that repeated devaluations have become an important contributant to the strato-inflationary process itself. Indeed in Argentina — as perhaps in Chile — it is probable that big devaluations set off the process in the first place because of the internal redistribution of income they caused.[3]

(1) The Latin American picture is, of course, clouded by the inclusion of countries with intrinsically unstable price-movements, which do have *some* effects in neighbouring economies.

(2) That is to say that these six countries show on average only 4 significant positive correlations and 3 significant negative correlations apiece — out of the 73 possible connections between their domestic price-movements and those in other countries which our matrix permits any one country to have. (There are other 'strato-inflationary' countries — in Asia — but their data is inadequate to include in the matrix.)

(3) A.G. Ford, *The Gold Standard 1880–1914: Britain and Argentina*, (Oxford 1962): 'In Argentina the economic and political structure was such that a depreciating paper currency (in terms of gold) moved the distribution of a given real income in favour of these (the landowning and exporting) interests and against wage-earners, both rural and urban.' pp. 90–91.

Thus the international links between national price-movements which are forged by world trade and competition have several implications. For instance, just as the world pattern shows that inflation over the whole of the post-war period cannot be exclusively structuralist-social (with the latter form's attendant patterns of expectations and anticipations), because it has been going on for quite a long time without escalating markedly, and has frequently slowed as well as accelerated, so equally the international linkage among industrial countries shows that inflation cannot in general be of the monetary-expenditure type. Unless, that is, one postulates a high degree of complementarity in national expansions in the money supply; and there is evidence that these work inversely — one country's domestic credit expansion being another's contraction.

This does not, however, imply that an international acceleration might not be set off by a monetary or fiscal indiscretion by a major trading economy. These fairly close international links, particularly for the industrial economies, mean not only that the domestic price increase is, for the 'normally-inflationary' group, restrained by international competition, but also that it is *tolerated* by international inflation. Thus if any major trading nation permits an accelerated inflation this may create 'room' for the others to inflate more as well.[1] Nevertheless, international price connections still act as a regulator of the process. If particular economies attempt to escape this regulation by successive devaluations, the internal effects may be such that they will move over into the strato-inflationary process, an involvement from which (as we have shown) it is extremely difficult to retreat.

Thus any arrangement which makes it easier for individual countries to tolerate national inflation makes it more likely that economies will change from an equilibrium process of inflation to a disequilibrium process. Under the system of fixed exchange rates which operated for most countries until the late 1960's, international competition was a major regulator of national price-levels. But if recent events (particularly the floating of the dollar and the pound in 1971/2) signify that a widespread system of semi-flexible, semi-floating rates may now be maintained, any shock which disturbs the 'normal', equilibrium system of inflation is likely to lead the countries affected into a process of disequilibrium or strato-inflation.

## Shocks, cycles and hyper-inflation

So far we have dealt in terms of two world systems of inflation, which are separated not merely by a statistical gulf (Graph II, again) but also by a

(1) Cf. Edgren, Faxén, and Odhner, *loc. cit.* That is, our model of wage-productivity price inflation needs now to be extended to take account of the fact that international price increases in the internationally competitive and fast productivity growth sector may provide an extra margin for wage increases over and above the *relevant* domestic productivity increase. Letting $T$ stand for trading prices we have instead of (5) (in p. 26, n. 1):

$$\left(\frac{\overline{\Delta p}}{p}\right) = \left(\frac{\Delta p}{p}\right)_T + \left(\frac{\Delta v}{v}\right)^* \Sigma a_i \frac{V_i}{V} - \left(\frac{\overline{\Delta v}}{v}\right) \qquad (9)$$

socio-economic one — such that an approach to its margins by any partici-
pant country is braked, often by economic crises, but particularly by intensified social conflict, with its concomitant of industrial unrest and political
instability. But countries *have* moved from equilibrium inflation to strato-
inflation, even in the two decades or so that are covered by our analysis.
Uruguay, for instance, only appears to have moved definitely into the strato-
inflationary group of economies towards the end of the 1950's; and there are
one or two apparently similar cases in Asian economies for which the statistical record was too uncertain to be used in our analyses. These are
certainly countries which have been teetering on the gulf's brink in recent
years: Colombia and Peru, for instance, but also Ghana, Turkey, Uganda.
These countries have all experienced one or two phases when the annual
rise in prices has significantly exceeded 10 per cent, and constitute most
of the upper edge of our band of 'normal' inflation in Graph II — a position
to which they have clearly had difficulty in holding. What kind of shocks
may push an economy over the brink?

One possibility is, of course, an exaggerated boom during the upswing of
the normal business cycle (which, as we noted in the previous section,
still makes a seeming impact on the world statistical record). And this
chance may be strengthening with time, particularly for the industrial market
economies, because institutional experience (in firms, unions, etc.) of the
effects of previous booms and recessions is accumulating into a diminished
respect for the latter. Which means that in the industrial countries the 'floor'
to 'normal' price inflation may be rising (a phenomenon not unconnected
with the successively increasing volumes of unemployment and excess
capacity which governments find necessary to confine rising prices), so that
the base from which boom wage and price movements start becomes higher.

However, we have no instance of an economy being pushed into chronic
disequilibrium inflation for such a cause as yet. But in any case, the cyclical
movements in the world economy are no longer to be construed as existing
independently of the swings in economic policy on the part of major governments. Indeed, it could well be argued that the cyclical movement in prices,
employment and production is now largely a product of the lagged and
variable response of major economies to changes in their own governments'
general economic policy — a responsive characteristic which in turn causes
governments first to over-act in one direction, then to over-compensate in the
other way, as they strive to regulate the general level of income and activity.
But this process is equally not exempt from political considerations and
pressures. And political pressures are quite another matter: one could cite
many cases where these have pushed individual countries into wage-price
spirals, from which they have subsequently found it difficult or impossible
to retreat.

A particular example of political effects is what the authors of the present
paper have called in another connection the 'Election Cycle'.[1] Graph V

(1) 'Wage Inflation and the Election Cycle' *The Times* (London), 24 March, 1970.

48

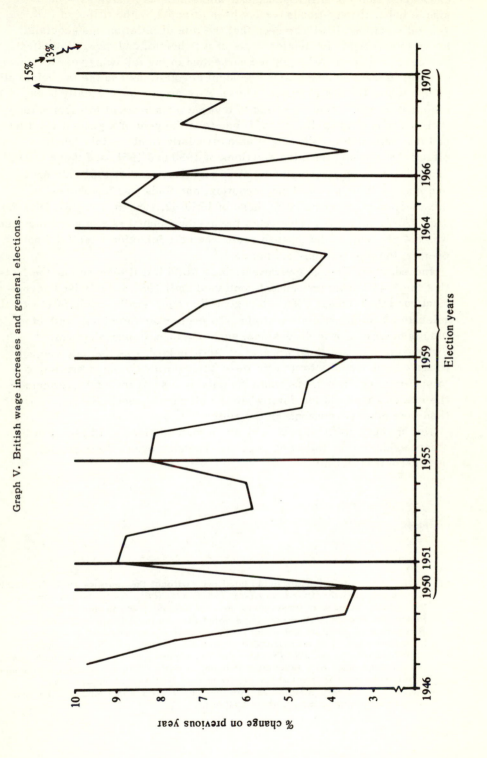

Graph V. British wage increases and general elections.

% change on previous year

Election years

15%
13%

49

shows how changes in British manual workers' hourly earnings — the best simple index of wage-trends — have been affected by the timing of U.K. general elections. It will be seen that the rate of inflation has generally begun to accelerate in election years or just before, and though the effect has commonly continued or gained momentum in the following year (because of the time taken in successive sectional negotiations and the lag before other groups follow the initial wage-leaders), governments have usually been reluctant to take definitive action to reverse the movement too soon after their success at the polls. Thus, if one take the year of a general election and that immediately following it as particularly liable to this 'election effect', but counts (since the elections of 1950 and 1951, and those of 1964 and 1966, were only separated by some eighteen months) 1951 only once and ignores 1967 in partial compensation, one finds five 'up-phases' of this election cycle since 1946: those of 1950/52, 1955/6, 1959/60, 1964/66 and 1970/71. In these twelve years the average annual rate of wage increase was 8.4 per cent; in the thirteen years when the 'election effect' did not operate, the rate was only 5.9 per cent. [1]

Indeed, every British government since World War II — reckoning the facts that the 1945 Labour government continued until 1951 and the 1964 government continued through 1966 — has gone through a similar cycle of electoral relaxation and intermediate restraint — a cycle which is clearly reflected also in other economic dimensions, such as those of unemployment. [2] Sir Winston Churchill's government of 1951, indeed, was the only one not to make some formal attempt at a wage/price policy (being committed to 'a bonfire of controls'), and was also notably less successful in bringing the rate of wage-inflation down when the electoral honeymoon was over than were other governments in the period.

Nor are such political cycles by any means confined to Britain. For instance again, on the following page are the dates of new Presidential administrations in Chile:

(1) Much the same relationship holds good even without the years of 1970/71, which may be considered extraordinary (see *The Times, ibid*). As to the reasons for the special increase in those years, see the second study in this Occasional Paper. But academic observers have noted the closing attempt by Mr. Wilson's government to prove its industrial relations policy a success by abandoning its incomes policy as a critical factor; and Mr. Heath's pre-election support for the doctors' campaign to restore the 30 per cent increase in pay which had been recommended by a favourable tribunal in early 1970, but partially suspended as too much even for the Labour government in that year to accept, was symbolic of the early attitude of the new Conservative administration. Its half-promise was, appropriately, about half-kept.

(2) Cf. *The Times, ibid.*

1932 Alessandri (snr.)
1938 Cerda (died in office)
1942 Rios (died in office)
1946 Videla
1952 Ibanez
1958 Alessandri (jnr.)
1964 Frei
1970 Allende

If these are compared with the record in Graph III of the Chilean annual rate of inflation since 1930, it will be seen that (with the exception of Sr. Allende, who has not yet had time to achieve a 'trough') every government in the period has been associated with one peak and one trough in the series, although the intervals between elections are longer than in the British case.[1]

Thus what governments and parties see as their short-run political necessity is itself a major determinant of fluctuations around the long-run rate of inflation. And such pressures have not infrequently pushed an economy over the boundary that divides one variety of inflation from a more severe form: clearly, the British political situation was a significant factor in pushing the economy dangerously near the brink of strato-inflation in 1970/71.[2]

To some extent associated with the political instability is another factor that has operated recently in some industrial economies (which are, however, of special significance both because of their general influence on world economic trends and because, as we noted, the recent inflationary upswing has only been unusually accentuated in the industrialised countries). This is the growing impact of direct taxation on employment incomes, which is tending to de-stabilise 'normal inflation' in a way which we analyse in our second study.[3]

(1) For a similar effect in Turkey, see Jackson, 'The Political Economy of Collective Bargaining, etc.' *loc. cit.*

(2) The role of decimalisation in this process has also yet to be fully explored; it may have contributed to the inflationary 'shock'. Ominously, the British economy has yet to face both entry to the Common Market and the introduction of the Value Added Tax.

(3) We can, however, extend our previous formalisation of the inflationary process (p. 47, n. 1), by supposing that if the marginal tax bite becomes too onerous for the wage-earner he will seek recompense in his gross wage demand. Let THP stand for take-home pay, $m$ for the marginal rate of taxation, $x$ for the average rate of taxation, and $w$ for gross earnings. Then the worker seeks an increase in his take home pay which will at the very least compensate for a rise in prices:

or

$$\left(\frac{\Delta \text{THP}}{\text{THP}}\right) = \frac{\Delta w (1 - m)}{w (1 - x)} = \frac{\Delta p}{p} \tag{10}$$

$$\frac{\Delta w}{w} = \frac{\Delta p}{p} \frac{(1 - x)}{(1 - m)} \tag{11}$$

With a marginal tax rate above the average tax rate, the wage demand has to be a multiple of the rate of price increase if take-home pay is even to keep up with rises in prices.

Perhaps particularly, there is the possibility of external shocks, from international price movements. There is at least a suggestion in the series for one or two Latin American economies that the factor that finally pushed them into a disequilibrium, strato-inflationary condition was the world price rise of 1951. Similarly, the unusually accelerated inflation of the industrial market economies over 1968/71 could be argued to be at least in part a reaction to the British, French, and consequent devaluations of 1967/8. While the latters' immediate effect, of course, was to tighten the competitive restraint on inflation in other industrial countries, at a second stage they both raised internal consumer prices in the devaluing countries and created more 'room' there for wage increases by a favourable effect on the national balance of payments. But these in turn set off a tertiary string of wage-price and wage-wage disturbances which contributed — certainly in the British case — to the 'wage explosion' of 1970.

However, among these various potential destabilisers, the political factor appears to remain central — at least in terms of the varying capacities of governments to master the sundry pressures involved (including those of the politicians' own short-run interests). Another problem with our objective classification of adequately recorded post-war inflations into two groups is that in theory (to revert) the possible gamut of trends in national price-levels ought to range from negative or zero movement to 'hyper-inflation' — which may perhaps be defined as a condition in which people are no longer willing to hold their national currency. Does our Graph II, for instance, mean that hyper-inflation is no longer a realistic possibility for post-War II economies?

The answer is that several instances of hyper-inflation have occurred, though the price record of the countries concerned is in consequence too disturbed or uncertain to include in such general analyses as those of this study's earlier sections. The conflict in Korea pushed that country into a virtual hyper-inflation in 1951, with consumer price-indices rising as follows (for the South):

|  | 1949 | 1950 | 1951 |
|---|---|---|---|
| % change on previous year | 50 | 167 | 350 |

In this case, the rate of inflation was subsequently reduced to a merely strato-inflationary process.[1] Similarly, revolution and secession caused a rise of prices recorded as 930 per cent for 1949 in what was then Formosa. However, war and revolution are not the only circumstances which may produce hyper-inflation.

The classic post-war case of that condition is the Indonesian, where prices rose over 300 per cent in 1965 and more than 1000 per cent in 1966. For what it is worth,[2] the statistical record of that event's background and upshot may be set out as in Table 10.

(1) On the tribulations and successes of stabilisation policies in Korea, see, S. Kanesa-Thasan, 'Stabilizing an Economy — A Study of the Republic of Korea'. *International Monetary Fund Staff Papers*, March 1969.

(2) Indonesian data is probably not very reliable, so these figures make no pretence to precision. However, their main course, and purport, seem unchallenged.

Table 10. *Indonesia: inflation, money supply and government finance*

| Annual Average: | Increase in Prices % | Increase in Money Supply[a] % | Ratio of Government Expenditure to Revenue |
|---|---|---|---|
| 1949—56 | 18 | 21 | 1.2 |
| 1957—58 | 28 | 48 | 1.4 |
| 1959—61 | 28 | 33 | 1.3 |
| 1962—64 | 133 | 118 | 2.1 |
| 1965—68 | 411 | 318 | 1.9 |
| 1969—71 | 7 | 40 | 1.3 |

[a] Currency plus bank deposits

*Sources*: E.C.A.F.E., *Economic Bulletin*: I.M.F. *International Financial Statistics*.

Up to 1962, the Indonesian Republic was respectably strato-inflationary, though it moved dangerously near the upper limit of that condition in 1958, after the nationalisation of Dutch enterprises led to both an expansion of the civil service and a sharp fall in the national income (partly consequent on the Dutch withdrawal from coastal and inter-island shipping). And an attempted monetary reform in 1959 produced so severe a deflationary shock that the banks were allowed to expand credit freely to restore the money supply.

But from 1962 the government placed impossible burdens on the budget by an expansion of military spending: there was the campaign for West Irian in 1962, the 'confrontation' with Malaysia in 1962 and the defeat of an attempted left wing coup in 1965 which was followed by widespread suppressive measures.[1] These things led to disruption of trade, international assistance and production on the one hand; on the other hand the government financed its inflated spending (apart from military expenditure, public salaries were doubled in 1963, and it seems clear that all central control over public departmental spending subsequently broke down) first by bank credit and finally by simply printing money.[2] During 1966 and 1967, President Sukarno was deprived of his powers, and a military regime progressively took control of the country. However, since military salaries were a major factor in the hyper-inflation, it was not for some years that this was cut back (partly under external pressure) to a superficially normal rate.[3]

(1) H. Myint, *Southeast Asia's Economy: Development Policies in the 1970s* (Penguin, 1972) pp. 34 ff. also attributes a large role in the subsequent economic collapse to the extirpation of the Chinese business community. A useful, if slightly biased, guide to the period is J.M. Pluvier, *Confrontations: a study in Indonesian Politics* (Oxford University Press, Kuala Lumpur, 1965).

(2) At the end of October, 1965, a KLM plane was chartered to fly 18 tons of currency notes from Paris to Djakarta, reported the Economist Intelligence Unit.

(3) P. Polomka, *Indonesia since Sukarno* (Penguin, 1971), especially ch. 6.

Thus the key feature of hyper-inflation is not so much the shock of war or rebellion — from which governments in other countries have emerged without the total collapse of confidence in the currency which it implies — but a political incapacity of government to dominate the forces pushing towards that condition. However, this might equally apply to transitions from a normal to a strato-inflationary state.

### Suppressed inflation: and a general view

Hyper-inflation is, from its nature, a transitory condition. It is economically and socially intolerable, as inconsistent with the maintenance of a money-exchange economy; and if the government cannot master it, the government will be overthrown. But by way of rounding off the picture, perhaps it is worth taking a brief glance at the other end of the spectrum of world experience in movements of price levels since the Second World War.

As our Graph II showed, the only economies, for which internationally-accepted indices of retail price movements are available, that appear to have experienced comparative price stability — at least since the early 1950's — are communist states.[1] One or two less developed countries show occasional periods of stable or even falling prices, but this is probably an effect of limited national price indices which are dominated by local foods; very good harvests thus pull down prices exceptionally, just as bad harvests push them up abnormally.

But the apparent price-stability of the planned economies (which, in substance, we accept as an approximate fact) is itself in some respects a puzzle. In the communist countries, wages and prices are important data of accountancy for national planning, and key levers in the allocation of man-power and productive resources between alternative uses. The state therefore has an interest in avoiding large or autonomous changes in the wage or price level. But these economies have also to absorb the effects of steadily rising productivity, and the rational way to arrange this is to compromise between falling prices and rising wages.

One reason for this is that *relative* prices have to change from time-to-time anyway, because both productivity and demand naturally change at different rates in the various branches of the economy, so it is sensible to combine the necessary adjustments of individual prices with reductions in the general price level which will pass some of the benefit of rising productivity on to the people as a whole. On the other hand, it is equally desirable that wages in general should be stable, granted that the wage-structure has already been arranged to guide different types of labour into the work where they can best be employed; if potential workers are to make a rational choice between

(1) Indices for a sufficient group of countries to be statistically analysable are only available from 1952. Scattered earlier data indicates greater variation before that date: e.g. there were very substantial price increases reported from Poland in 1950/52, and big price reductions from the U.S.S.R. in the same time. (There was, of course, also a rapid peace-time inflation in the Soviet Union before the Second World War).

alternative jobs they must be able to estimate the different life-time earnings which the available careers will offer, and it is difficult to do that if all wages are changing continually. But since the demands for and supplies of different types of labour (or for labour in different places, sectors and conditions) are themselves changing, it is also desirable to change relative wage-differentials from time to time; and the easiest way to do this is by selective increases in particular wage-rates. So the other part of the general increase in productivity is taken up by a rise in the *average* wage-level.

But this combination of steadily rising average wages with steadily falling average prices is far from being one that the communist economies have achieved (as Graph VI suggests — even though, since this is also an average of national experiences, it understates the fluctuation in price movements of particular countries.[1] ). Thus, even if we exclude the early 1950's up to 1954, when there were fairly large changes in the price level — in both directions — for several countries,[2] the annual changes in average prices have varied (up or down, again) over a range of nearly 11 percentage points in Bulgaria, 5 in Hungary and nearly 8 in Poland. The range in the U.S.S.R. is smallest, at just over 3, and is decreasing most over time; but that country has also the longest experience in the management of prices and incomes. While the Graph for the six countries together even suggests a certain cyclical fluctuation in prices for the communist group.

This fluctuation, moreover, is to a large degree common to the several countries concerned. These were not included in the matrix of international connections between changes in national price-levels of which our Table 8 is a summary extract, but a separate matrix for the communist countries alone shows that consumer price-level variations in the economies covered by Graph VI are highly inter-correlated. Of all the possible pairs of national price-indices within the group, only one pair fails to yield a positive correlation which is statistically significant at the 95 per cent level of confidence; and an average coefficient of significant linkage between national price-movements in these six communist countries, calculated in the same way as those for Australia and Turkey previously suggested,[3] yields the very high figure of 0.603. So it appears that even in a planned economy, national price-movements are at least as much subject to external regulations and pressures as in the industrial market countries.[4]

(1) The six countries covered by the Graph are Bulgaria, Czechoslovakia, East Germany, Hungary, Poland, and the U.S.S.R.

(2) Alec Nove, *An Economic History of the U.S.S.R.* (Allen Lane The Penguin Press, 1969), ch. 11.

(3) See p. 43.

(4) For further consideration of this specific point, and for some support to our general argument, see J. Goldmann and K. Kouba, *Economic Growth in Czechoslovakia* (Academia Publishing House, Prague, 1969), ch. V.

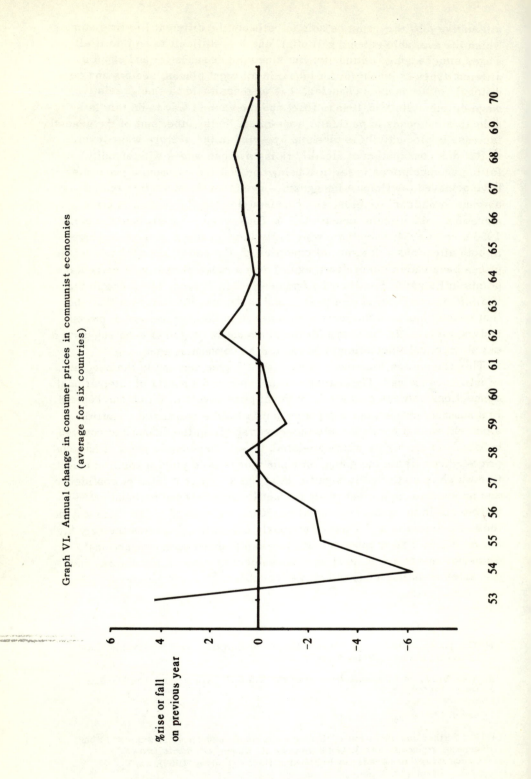

Graph VI. Annual change in consumer prices in communist economies
(average for six countries)

%rise or fall
on previous year

General price reductions have been fairly frequent acts of state policy in the communist countries. It seems equally clear, however, that there are a number of pressures which tend to push costs and prices up in an unplanned and unintended way. Obvious to any visitor to these economies is a shortage of many consumer goods at current prices and incomes — made apparent by occasional queues, special priority allocation systems (or even 'black markets') for some highly desired commodities, long waiting lists for, e.g. private cars even at very high prices, and so on. Limitations on educational and job choice constitute a virtual priority allocation system in the labour market. And there, another symptom is the undoubted existence of 'wage drift' (which in western countries many economists take as an indication of inflationary pressures), arising from such things as the effect of piece-rate and incentive schemes, the manipulation of authorised wage-bonuses by managements to attract or hold scarce varieties of labour or alleviate petty discontents, failures to realise planned production while planned wage-bills are spent, and so on;[1] these have a distorting impact on wage differentials that necessitates occasional major revisions of the wage-structure (again, with an average upward result) to correct it.

Perhaps the dominant factor, however, is the pervasive pressure to raise output. And even in planned economies, plans sometimes go wrong; the only way to anticipate such eventualities would be to hold a reserve of capacity which is not in continual use: and to keep an adequate reserve idle would be a luxury which the various demands on and ambitions for the economy will hardly allow. In sum, wage-costs tend to rise more than is planned, excess demand in various sectors reinforces this pressure, and prices are pushed up. The overall price trend for communist economies thus exhibits a certain see-saw movement, in which a tendency for prices to creep up is periodically offset by bouts of systematic price-reduction, often accompanied by other measures to keep costs under control (such as revisions of productive 'norms', of wage-payment and accountancy systems, etc.).[2]

What these economies appear to have, in other words, is not so much a state of price stability as one of immanent inflation suppressed by rigorous central controls. The example of Yugoslavia (where, the rate of annual increase in consumer prices, though averaging in the past twenty years rather less than 10 per cent, has tended to rise over time and from the late 1950's has fluctuated so widely that the country apparently borders on strato-inflation) suggests that a decentralised socialist economy would have great difficulty in controlling inflationary pressures.[3] While there has equally

(1) Cf. L.J. Handy, 'National Job Evaluation in the Soviet Union and Poland' D.A.E. Mimeo (to be published).

(2) Nove, *op. cit.* pp. 345 ff.

(3) On which point we disagree strongly with Jaroslav Vanek, *The General Theory of Labor-Managed Market Economies* and *The Participatory Economy* (Cornell University Press, 1970 and 1971). For further discussion of the problem, see, J.M. Fleming and V.S. Sertic, 'The Yugoslav Economic System', *International Monetary Fund Staff Papers*, July 1962, esp. p. 212; Aleksander Bajt, 'Yugoslav Economic Reforms, Monetary and Production Mechanism', *Economics of Planning*, Vol. 7, No. 3, 1967; and L. Sirc, 'Inflation in Jugoslavia', *Review of the Study Center of Yugoslav Affairs*, No. 5.

been at least one case in the post-war world where a non-communist (indeed, highly anti-communist) government which was comparatively unencumbered by overt political conflict and the pressures of organised social groups has mastered and suppressed a previously very high inflationary rate. In Taiwan, the Chiang Kai-Shek regime brought the increase in prices down, from the hyper-inflation of 1949 and 1950 which has already been referred to, first to the lower edge of a mere strato-inflation (with the annual rate averaging around 15 per cent in the rest of the 1950's), and then to very near absolute price stability in the early 1960's: from 1961 to 1966 the reported average annual increase in retail prices was 1.2 per cent. This situation was apparently too much to maintain in face of Taiwan's external connections and internal boom, but the country has since remained well within the 'equilibrium' band.[1]

If this view of price-movements in the planned economies is accepted as substantially correct, then the entire world experience of price-trends since the late 1940's can be comprised in four distinct levels or varieties. First, there is 'suppressed inflation': a condition mainly characteristic of certain communist countries, in which upward pressures on incomes and costs are repeatedly corrected by internal controls and adjustments — and to some extent regulated by close trading connections within the East European Communist bloc — so that price-levels fluctuate around a zero rate of change.

Second, the industrial capitalist economies have so far experienced what we earlier called normal or 'equilibrium' inflation: in the major sectors of fast productivity growth, prices are not reduced and wages rise as fast as per capita output, so that in other sectors wages necessarily rise more than productivity, and average prices persistently increase. And the system has been further kept to a fairly steady path — until very recently — by international trade and competition. So that although annual rates of inflation fluctuate with business and 'political' cycles, they have tended to do so around a moderate 3 per cent or so. This system has also been characteristic of most of the developing countries, except that (as one might expect) they show on the average rather greater variation around the 'equilibrium' path.

The third level or form of inflation is 'strato-inflation' — a condition which has been best recorded for certain South American countries, but is not confined to them. Here, national price-increases have become detached from the 'normal' wage-productivity and international trade regulators: there are genuine and severe wage/price spirals, but these are also accompanied and accelerated by repeated and arbitrary redistributions of income between social groups. The system fluctuates between a 'panic' ceiling inflation rate around 50 per cent, and a 'floor' rate around 10 per cent, so that

---

(1) See S. Kawano, 'The Reasons for Taiwan's High Growth Rate' in the Committee for Economic Development, *Economic Development Issues: Greece, Israel, Taiwan and Thailand* (Praeger, New York, 1968) esp. p. 139.

prices *on average* have risen at close to 30 per cent a year. The condition is generally marked by severe socio-industrial conflict, high political instability and repeated external devaluations.

And finally there is hyper-inflation; a necessarily transitory state of affairs which nevertheless possesses several post-war examples. Hyper-inflations have reached an annual rate of price-increase around 1000 per cent: the total collapse of the national currency's value is invariably associated with a radical political collapse or disaster.

The four levels are thus also identified with distinctly different degrees of political and economic integration or stability, and of social and industrial conflict — ranging from the monolithic to the disintegrating state. And our preceding analyses will also indicate that a loss of social integration or political control at one level may push an economy from its accustomed condition of inflation to a radically more violent one. But this suggests a rather different view of the nature of persistent post-War II inflation from either of the main theoretical positions we outlined in this Study's initial discussion.

This view would include two central propositions. First, that inflation arises *neither* from monetary misdemeanours or mistakes on the part of fiscal authorities, *nor* from identifiable structural defects in the social economy — though either of these things may complicate and inflame the inflationary process — but is intrinsic to the modern economy itself: and this is true whether the economy be 'planned', 'industrial market' or merely 'developing' (to revert to the official U.N. typology). This proposition rests on the greatly increased importance of three phenomena. One is international trade, in which all economies are more or less involved. Another — and perhaps most significant — is the socio-economic role of governments. And the last is the development of non-governmental socio-economic organisations and institutions — including trade unions and professional associations, but also including farmers' associations, public or para-statal corporations, big private monopolies, conglomerates, oligopolistic and international firms, and employers' and businessmen's associations.

The effect of increased trade between countries needs little discussion. It implies that individual countries must either accept major external influences on the movement of domestic prices, or evade those influences at the cost of severe internal dislocation and disturbance.[1] The enormously increased importance of governments arises from several things — the impact of 'total war' from 1939 to 1945, the emergence and example of central planning in the socialist countries, the effect of Keynesian economies, the desire for national development and social improvement. At any rate, in nearly all countries a lion's share of the flow of economic resources is canalised through the state and its subsidiary agencies; and the government is almost

---

(1) The importance of the connection between the causes of inflation and the problem of international liquidity has consistently been emphasised by Thomas Balogh; see his paper 'International Reserves and Liquidity' *Economic Journal* June 1960.

universally regarded as having a central responsibility, not merely for the general evolution of the economy and society, but for a satisfactory progress in all aspects of economic and social affairs.[1]

But governments have many objectives. They want, for instance, to secure economic growth and prosperity, to maintain certain levels of military spending, to increase industrial and public investment, to expand employment, to preserve or extend various social expenditures, to adjust income distributions, as well as to achieve political stability and industrial peace — conditions which are commonly regarded as purchasable. Politicians want at least to hold on to state power, and bureaucracies to increase it. And Governments are not detached from interests, but are subject also to the pressure of organisations which are essentially 'demanding'. Ross long ago described trade unions as 'political agencies operating in an economic environment',[2] but this is equally true of large firms, business, professional and farmers' organisations.

Economic organisations, that is to say, are not simply institutional versions of hagglers in a market place where behaviour is dominated by every shift of local demand or supply, but also social organisations whose policy has to reconcile the ambitions of leaders with the conflicting interests of diverse internal groups. Their wage and price decisions are thus conditioned by factors which do not all relate to immediate labour and product market situations: and their participants see them also as vehicles for broader aims: they are expected to do such things as maintain and improve their members' real or relative standards of life and wealth, and fulfill sundry expectations aroused by a general condition of productive growth; they want — if not actual subsidies, tax concessions and similar advantages — state support and guarantees for policies, laws and mechanisms which will facilitate these aims.

All this adds up to the statement that demands on the contemporary economy inevitably exceed its capacity: a condition of which inflation is simply the monetary expression. Inflation, however, has many inconveniences: for instance, that it complicates the accountancy and prediction on which the economic behaviour of individuals and organisations is based,[3] introduces general uncertainty, and involves a risk of destructive runaway spirals of various kinds ('wage-price' and other); and for these inconveniences, governments will also be held responsible. But self-evidently, if our preceding statement has substance, it can only be held down if other demands on the economy are sacrificed, reconciled, moderated or suppressed.

---

(1) On this point, see Andrew Shonfield, *Modern Capitalism* (Oxford University Press, 1965).

(2) A.M. Ross, *Trade Union Wage Policy* (University of California Press, 1948); see the excerpt from this book reprinted in W.E.J. McCarthy (ed.), *Trade Unions* (Penguin, 1972).

(3) Michael Ward, *National Income and the Valuation of Stocks*, D.A.E. Occasional Paper No. 35 (Cambridge University Press, forthcoming) esp. ch. 4.

Which brings us to the second proposition: that the extent to which the economy's intrinsic inflationary tendency is in fact controlled depends on the political capacity and wisdom of governments (including that to deny themselves sundry devices and acts which offer short-term political or bureaucratic gain) and on their society's degree of integration, consensus or acquiescence on the part of its various economic groups. But this is a two-way process: a failure or inability to control or hold inflation will itself invoke a parallel degree of social conflict that will limit the government's power to keep back inflationary pressures.[1]

Thus in the communist economies, where overall national planning gives certainty and prediction a high priority, where the state holds most of the relevant economic levers, where autonomous economic associations operate within narrow limits, and where overt social conflict is inhibited, inflation is held to an average zero rate — though with many 'near-misses' and considerable technical difficulty: the optimal gradually declining price level has so far proven beyond their capacity.

The industrial capitalist economies are mostly 'pluralistic': that is to say, power is shared, in varying degrees, between the state and sundry autonomous institutions and organisations: moreover, political power is itself subject to a competition, of which the capacity to dispense benefits or largesse is an instrument. And inflation is incidentally a means by which social tensions and conflicts are temporarily but repeatedly eased.[2] So the priority of inflation control against other state objectives is lower and the difficulty of achieving it greater: indeed, a reduction of the normal rate of price increase — say by deflation (implying unemployment and bankruptcies) or severe wage/price controls — is as likely to intensify social conflict as is an acceleration of inflation. Governments will usually only take drastic action against the latter when some more central objective — the preservation of a necessary balance of foreign payments (or governmental continuity itself) — is threatened.

So, governments, firms, unions and other major interests in effect learn to live with inflation by conventionalising it. What we have called 'equilibrium' inflation is a social device which reconciles the self-concerns of the leading firms, those of dominant unions or interest associations, and the governmental stake in a viable external balance. Although this appears to be a simple statement, it nevertheless involves an elaborate complex of behavioural patterns; nor are these mechanisms precisely geared together, and so the economy is liable to cyclical fluctuations: while a major disturbance of them risks a breakdown of the equilibrium itself.

(1) On the manifold complex of economic conflict, a very good, and indeed the only, guide is Jan Pen, *Harmony and Conflict in Modern Society* (McGraw Hill, London, 1966).

(2) Jan Pen, *Income Distribution* (Allen Lane, The Penguin Press, 1971) chs. IV and VII.

We must emphasise, parenthetically, that it is only the dominant social groups who generally manage to keep ahead of rising prices; the less powerful and/or socially disadvantaged groups may suffer substantial hardship. To some extent their plight can be ameliorated by increased social security payments and other welfare benefits, but such a redistribution of income may be resisted by the dominant groups,[1] and thus the weaker sections of the community may be increasingly impoverished by inflation.[2]

The same broad analysis holds true for most of the developing countries, except that their 'pluralism' is far narrower in scope and many more people — typically, the subsistence farmers and the urban unemployed, at least — suffer deprivation through inflation. In these countries, therefore, the social and economic equilibrium is much more brittle.[3] And a collapse of the political balance may precipitate an economy into strato-inflation, where intensified social conflict limits the power of governments to do more than periodically pull back the society from the 'panic' rate at which conflicting group interests are temporarily subdued. If a government cannot do this, — conflict — and perhaps hyper-inflation — dominates until it is replaced by one that can.

In the upshot of these two propositions, then, a degree of fundamental validity is implied to both the main theoretical positions on the 'causes' of inflation which were outline at this Study's commencement. 'Monetary/ expenditure' theories state a central point, that demands on the contemporary economy invariably exceed supplies, of which persistent inflation is the monetary translation. And 'structural/social' theories reflect an equally vital consideration: that inflation is propagated, perpetuated and accelerated by mechanisms that are bound up with distortion of market processes and conflicts of social groups who create and move the stocks and flows comprising a modern economy. But if the source, mechanics and typology of inflation are such as our analysis has led us to infer, it would be as idle — indeed, as disastrous — to attribute responsibility to any single party to the process, as to rely on any single and simple remedy that ignored the phenomenon's inherent socio-economic complexity.

(1) 'For all men are by nature provided of notable multiplying glasses, that is their passions and self-love, through which, every little payment (of taxes) appeareth a great grievance; but are destitute of those prospective glasses, namely moral and civil science, to see afar off the miseries that hang over them, and cannot without such payments be avoided.' Thomas Hobbes, *Leviathan*, 1651, ch. XVIII. Hobbes' chapter thirteen also contains some remarks of more general relevance to the theory of inflation.

(2) This problem has been considered elsewhere by one of the present authors, and we here refrain from expanding this very important point; see Dudley Jackson, *Poverty* (Macmillan, London, 1972) and Dudley Jackson and Ann Fink, 'Assets, Liabilities and Poverty', *Social and Economic Administration*, October 1971.

(3) For a more detailed treatment of all these points, see H.A. Turner, *I.L.O. Reports, op. cit.*; and Dudley Jackson: 'Economic Development and Income Distribution in Eastern Africa', *Journal of Modern African Studies*, December 1971; and 'Wage Policy and Industrial Relations in India', *Economic Journal*, March 1972.

# 3. The wage-tax spiral and labour militancy

*(Frank Wilkinson and H.A. Turner)*

### Inflation, unemployment and strikes: two contradictions

Two major contradictions in economic and social trends have puzzled the analysts and theoretical students of these matters over the years since 1967. One is the coincidence of increasing unemployment in the market industrial countries with sharply accelerated wage-and-price inflation, which defied the previous (if quite recent) widespread acceptance by economists of theorems indicating that the rate of money wage increase and the level of unemployment were inversely correlated. The second is the parallel coincidence of substantially increased unemployment in several such countries with a quite dramatic upsurge of industrial unrest — measured in terms not merely of a much augmented incidence of "man-days of idleness" from labour disputes (say, in relation to the total employed population) but also in terms of a multiplied frequency of strikes. And this was surprising because historically the frequency of strikes has also varied inversely to the level of unemployment, so that — although labour stoppages might individually last longer or involve more workers when unemployment was high — the decline in their number meant that there was also no general tendency for the loss of working days to increase at such times.

Among economists, probably the most widely favoured explanation of the first contradiction was some selection or combination of propositions to the effect that the 'trade-off curve' between the level of unemployment and the rate of wage-increase had shifted, or that workers (and others) were increasingly anticipating future price inflation in their current wage and income demands.[1]

The difficulty with the former type of explanation is that the reasons so far advanced for the shift in the Phillips Curve are not wholly convincing, or of general application to the countries affected.[2] The problem with the other type of explanation is that (as our first study showed) inflation has

---

(1) For good recent examples of the main alternative approaches, see Charles L. Schultze, 'Has the Phillips Curve Shifted? Some additional Evidence', and William Fellner, 'Phillips-type Approach or Acceleration?' both in *Brookings Papers on Economic Activity*, 2, 1971 (Brookings Institute, Washington).

(2) For instance, the structural change in the composition of the unemployed which is very intelligently argued by George Perry (Brookings Papers, 3, 1970) could be as much a product as a cause of the U.S. shift, and would not necessarily apply to other countries.

been almost continuous in many countries for over thirty years, and has on one or two previous occasions also accelerated to a rate, at a world level, quite comparable with that reached in 1970/71. It is not at all clear why trade unions (for instance) should only so recently have 'learned' to assume inflation as normal, or why (if the previous accelerations of inflation were also associated with increased expectations of that phenomenon's continuance) they should have subsequently 'unlearned' to do so. Moreover, it is a difficulty with both explanations that — as our first study again showed — it is only in the industrial 'market' economies that the recent accentuation of the rate at which prices rose was at all abnormal by comparison with previous oscillations in this rate, so that to the extent that a special explanation is required, it must relate specifically to them.

Explanations of the second contradiction have been more diverse, ranging from the 'demonstration effect' of the student and labour unrest in France in 1968, through the impact of the devaluation of national currencies in 1967/68 on real wages, to the collapse of the British Labour Government's incomes policy and planned industrial relations legislation in 1969. However, these suggestions suffer above all from their national specificity: they do not explain why the increased incidence of labour stoppages should have been so general.[1]

Our two contradictions are clearly linked — certainly by the increase in unemployment, and at least presumably by some more than accidental association between heightened industrial unrest and accelerated inflation. It would therefore be an advantage to their explanation to adduce some causal factor which was common between them.

The treatment of wages in discussion of these questions has historically dealt in trends of money wages or real wages — in the sense of employees' gross earned income after allowing for changes in their living costs. This study suggests that, because the steady increase in wages in the market industrial countries has pushed a rising proportion of workers into the net of generally progressive tax systems, trends in *net* real wages — i.e. after allowing for direct tax and related deductions as well as for price changes — may now be the more relevant parameter of reference. The data of the following is drawn from Great Britain; but there is evidence of similar trends, situations and relationships in other countries, and particularly the United States.

(1) For instance, Professor Hugh Clegg's booklet 'How to Run an Incomes Policy: and Why We Made Such a Mess of the Last One' (Heinemann, 1971) while it carefully avoids explicit casual attributions for the British uprush, nevertheless clearly associates its onset with pay inequities under the preceding incomes policy, and its severity with institutional changes in collective bargaining. And one of the present authors (H.A. Turner, 'Collective Bargaining and the Eclipse of Incomes Policy, etc.', *British Journal of Industrial Relations*, July, 1970) attributed the breakdown of the Labour Government's wages policy to similar factors. But neither of these considerations apply to the United States, where the incidence of strikes rose just as much.

## Deductions from wages: post-war trends in real net income

In Britain there are two important direct deductions from the wage-earner's pay — income tax (surtax is levied additionally on higher incomes which are, however, still virtually above the wage-earning income brackets) and social insurance contributions. Various forms of 'negative income tax' — subventions to people with very small incomes — are increasingly important, but these all apply to people in special circumstances (such as low-income tenants of public housing); and the most general — the Family Income Supplement — was introduced only in August 1971. Small family allowances are payable to parents with more than one child, but these are taxable. Income tax is currently levied at a standard rate on all income above a figure determined for each taxpayer by various exemption 'allowances' based on personal circumstances and the proportion of income which is earnt, though until 1970 there were 'reduced rates' of tax which rose in steps from that figure to a higher one at which the standard rate became payable. Social insurance contributions consist of a flat-rate deduction for all employees (except married women who may opt out if their husbands are earning) plus, since 1961, a 'graduated pension' contribution which varies with income up to a certain level of the latter.[1]

Table 1* shows what has happened to the gross annual income (estimated from the regular official enquiry into manual workers' earnings in a week of October each year[2]), deductions from pay, and net real income of an average wage-earner in typical circumstances, at four-yearly intervals from 1948 — except that the 1970 figures are given separately. (Provisional figures are also included for 1971, for which year the appropriate earnings data has not yet been published at time of writing). Table 2* converts the trends shown by the first table into annual rates of change.

It will be seen that the typical manual worker was hardly liable for income tax until the late 1950's, and that even in 1960 his tax and social insurance contributions together took less than 8 per cent of his earnings. In 1970/71, however, this proportion had risen to nearly 20 per cent.

Table 2* shows how sharply the effect of these deductions has increased in more recent years. Over the whole period from 1948 to 1970, gross money earnings rose at an average annual rate of about 6½ per cent, increasing prices reduced the real value of this to 2½ per cent, and taxes cut it again to 1½ per cent. But whereas up to the mid-1950's the tax effect was negligible, from 1964 to 1970 these deductions took back the lion's share of the workers' annual increase in real income.

This rising trend of wage-taxation can be confirmed by an alternative calculation, which is of interest incidentally because it also begins to indicate how the trend has borne differently on different groups of workers. Table 3* conveys similar estimates for *all* employees.

(1) A more detailed note on changes in income tax and social insurance contributions is included in Appendix A.

(2) Detailed references for the data in this Paper's Graphs and Tables are given in Appendix B.

Table 1* *Gross money income (£s per annum), direct taxes and net income of average wage earner — married with two children under eleven*

|       | Gross income | Tax (P.A.Y.E.) | National Insurance and Graduated Contributions | Net income | Net real income (1948 prices) |
|-------|------|------|------|------|------|
| 1948  | 372  | 0    | 13   | 359  | 359  |
| 1952  | 485  | 0    | 15   | 470  | 372  |
| 1956  | 640  | 6    | 18   | 616  | 425  |
| 1960  | 777  | 25   | 26   | 726  | 462  |
| 1964  | 963  | 43   | 50   | 870  | 486  |
| 1968  | 1243 | 137  | 67   | 1039 | 496  |
| 1970  | 1505 | 214  | 86   | 1206 | 509  |
| 1971[a] | 1655 | 215 | 96   | 1344 | 519  |

[a] Provisional

Table 2* *Rates of growth in gross money, real and net real income, men manual workers*

| Annual compound rate of growth | a Gross money income | b Gross real income | c Net real income | Price effect a—b | Tax effect b—c |
|-------|------|------|------|------|------|
| (%)   |      |      |      | Percentage Points | |
| 1948—52 | 6.9  | 0.6  | 0.7  | 6.2  | −0.1 |
| 1952—56 | 7.2  | 3.6  | 3.5  | 3.6  | 0.2  |
| 1956—60 | 5.0  | 2.9  | 2.1  | 2.1  | 0.8  |
| 1960—64 | 5.5  | 2.2  | 1.3  | 3.3  | 0.9  |
| 1964—68 | 6.6  | 2.5  | 0.5  | 4.1  | 2.0  |
| 1968—70 | 10.0 | 3.6  | 1.3  | 6.4  | 2.3  |
| 1970—71[a] | 10.0 | 0.5 | 1.9 | 9.5 | −1.4 |

[a] Provisional

There is not a great deal of difference in the movement of gross money earnings as between men manual workers and all employees, except perhaps for the period 1952—56 (that manual wages grew faster than salary earnings between 1950 and 1955 has been shown by Routh[1] ). In general terms, the calculations for all employees otherwise show much the same effects as those in Tables 1* and 2*. There is a similar marked increase in the proportion of income taken as tax and social insurance contributions. Particularly, the annual rate of growth in net real income reached a peak for both groups in the mid-1950's, and thereafter declined.

However, over the whole period of these tables, net real income apparently increased, on the whole, rather faster for all employees than for men wage-earners — at rather over 2 per cent annually, nearly one-third as much again

(1) Guy Routh, 'Occupation and Pay in Great Britain, 1906—60' (C.U.P. 1965, p. 126). Dept. of Employment indices for manual workers' and salaried employees' earnings indicate that salaries then rose faster until 1960, after which wages began to gain once more. However, wage-earnings there refer to *all* manual workers.

Table 3* *Gross money income, direct taxes and net income, all employees, with rates of growth*

| (i) £ per annum | Gross money income | Income taxes and National Insurance | Net money income | Net real income (1948 prices) |
|---|---|---|---|---|
| 1948 | 303 | 28 | 275 | 275 |
| 1970 | 1183 | 220 | 963 | 447 |

| (ii) Rates of growth (% p.a.) in: | a Gross money income | b Net real income | Contributions to % points difference between a & b | |
|---|---|---|---|---|
| | | | Price effect | Tax effect |
| 1948—52 | 6.7 | 1.6 | 5.1 | 0.0 |
| 1952—56 | 6.5 | 3.5 | 3.1 | 0.0 |
| 1956—60 | 4.8 | 2.3 | 2.1 | 0.5 |
| 1960—64 | 5.6 | 2.0 | 3.1 | 0.5 |
| 1964—68 | 6.4 | 1.2 | 3.9 | 1.3 |
| 1968—70 | 10.2 | 3.4 | 5.5 | 1.3 |

as the increase for male manual workers alone. This difference arises partly from the different price indices used. In estimating manual workers' real earnings we have taken the Index of Retail Prices, which is designed mainly to reflect the cost of wage-earners' consumption, whereas for all employees it seemed more appropriate to reckon from the general index of prices of consumers' goods and services which is constructed from National Income estimates. The former index includes a larger proportion of food and housing expenditure, so the difference reflects a real divergence in the consumption costs of different social groups.

But the second reason for the apparent divergence in income trends between wage-earners and other employees is that increases in the gross real income of men manual workers were subject to a greater 'clawback' for income tax and social insurance levies. This did not happen because men wage-earners' average earnings were higher: what reduces the gross money income average for all employees is the large proportion of female workers these include. But these have, on the whole, smaller tax-exemption allowances because they support fewer dependents and include many married women; so that the average tax liability constitutes a similar proportion of total income both for men manual workers and for all employees together. However, the 'personal allowances' themselves exempted a steadily declining proportion of income from tax as earnings rose, and other changes in the tax incidence also implied a greater deduction from men wage-earners' incomes than those of other workers.

Finally, increases in the net real income of all employees did not fall to such a low rate as those of men manual workers during 1964—68, and re-covered much more sharply in the following two years — again, as comparison of the Tables shows, largely effects of differential marginal tax incidences. Both series, however display the common characteristic that, whereas up to the mid 1950's it was increases in living costs that were responsible for reducing the value of workers' monetary gains, from then on direct taxes represent a very significant offset to increases in workers' real income.

Further comparison of the two series, moreover, reveals one further aspect of taxation's post-war impact on employment incomes. Graph I* shows the the trends of a typical man wage-earners' income and the average income of all employees over the whole period from 1948 to 1970 (the latest date for which estimates for both categories can be made). Although a moving average is used to bring out the general movement, the graph shows the beginning of the 1970 wage-explosion. It also shows, however, how far gross money changes in income may mislead as to real and relative trends. Thus the similar wage-explosion of the early 1950's affected only manual workers' pay substantially — the trend in gross money earnings of all employees remained fairly level. Yet in terms of net real income increases there was little difference between the two groupings. The black segment in each figure represents the increasing impact of state deductions, and this is visibly greater for men manual workers than for all workers together. (Since about half of these are themselves men wage-earners, the impact on *other* groups of employed people must have been significantly less again).

Especially, however, the second diagram shows that the rising state clawback from work incomes is not just a change from a condition of tax-neutrality towards wage and salary increases, but an actual reversal of previous tax-effects. Up to the mid-1950's, tax changes (represented here by the white segment of tax reductions in the lower left-hand corner of diagram b) were actually offsetting increases in living costs for all employees, not adding to those increases' effect on real living standards.

### Factors in increased wage-taxation

There have been two factors in the increasing incidence of direct taxation on employment incomes. One was the effect of changes in government tax policy. The other — and on the whole more important — has been the effect of general income increases themselves, within a direct tax system in which increments of income are taxed at successively higher rates. This has, indeed, often had the result that changes in tax scales have produced quite different actual effects to those apparently intended by the government which made them.

The clearest example of deliberately increased direct taxation is that of social insurance contributions, which — as Table 1* shows — represented about 3 per cent of men manual workers' average income throughout the 1950's, but then grew to some 6 per cent in 1970/71. The 'flat-rate' item in the National Insurance levy on employees was increased six times between 1960 and 1970, almost doubling in cash. In 1961, however, a 'graduated pension' scheme, designed to relate state retirement benefits to earnings during working life, was introduced and later extended to other benefits. This scheme required contributions varying according to weekly earnings, within a range from £9 to £15 of the latter. By 1970 the upper earnings limit of this range had been raised to £30 per week, with related extensions to the progressive scale of contributions; moreover, the contribution rates themselves

Graph I* Trends[a] in rates of increase of average gross money, gross real, and net real income, 1948—1970

(a) Manual worker, wife and two children (D.E.P. Enquiry)

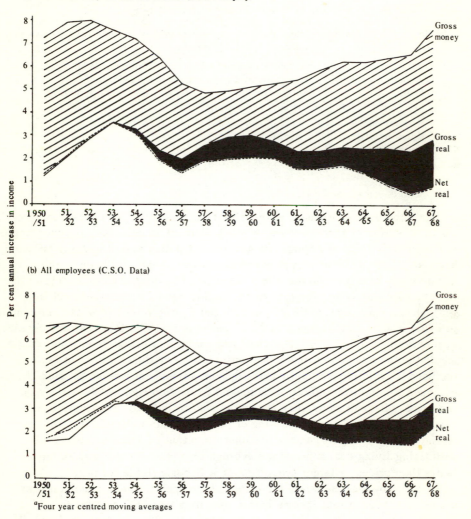

(b) All employees (C.S.O. Data)

[a]Four year centred moving averages

had been raised three times. The increased social insurance deductions thus represented a combination of 'policy' increases and additions designed to maintain the real value of benefits and contributions in face of inflation.

Curiously enough, however, the effect of the graduated benefit scheme is not to make the social insurance contributions into a progressive tax. As Table 4[*] shows, the high flat rate element combines with the earnings' ceiling to ensure that the percentage of income taken by the contribution continues smaller as one moves up the earnings range. The new scheme did, however, make the contribution system a little less regressive at middling or moderately high levels of wages (Table 4[*] again), but this effect disappears as one moves out of wage-incomes' normal range.

Table 4[*] *Social insurance contributions as percentages of various levels of men manual workers' earnings*

| Relative income level | National insurance and graduated pension as % earnings | | Increase 1960 to 1970 (percentage points) |
|---|---|---|---|
| | 1960 | 1970 | |
| Highest decile | 2.5 | 4.4 | 1.9 |
| Upper quartile | 3.0 | 5.3 | 2.3 |
| Median | 3.6 | 6.0 | 2.4 |
| Lower quartile | 4.5 | 6.4 | 1.9 |
| Lowest decile | 5.4 | 7.2 | 1.8 |

*Source* See Appendix B.

The 'progressive' element in the direct tax system is, of course, income tax (plus surtax at higher income levels). Here, it is less easy to disentangle the separate effects of changes in government policy and of general inflation, because in the post-war period governments have generally been in the apparent position of *reducing* direct taxation. The only obvious exception is the standard rate of income tax which, having been progressively cut from its high war-time level to 38.75 per cent per £, was raised to 41.25 per cent in 1965: it was reduced again to 38.75 per cent in 1971. However, successive governments increased the 'personal' and children's allowances which determined the tax exemption limits, and adjusted the 'reduced rates' of tax or the band to which these applied (though the adjustment was sometimes designed to offset the effect of increased exemption limits). Nevertheless the actual effect of many such decisions was to increase the relative incidence of taxation. Thus the raising of personal and children's allowances on the average, roughly, and in the long run adjusted these to keep pace with rising living costs: but since average employee income was rising faster than prices, a larger proportion of it became liable for tax.

We can, however, separate the effect of changes in the tax incidence at a *constant* level of real income before tax, from that of *increases* in real income on tax liability with a *given* tax structure. This is done in Graph II[*]: this compares the effect of the income tax structure of 1960 (shown as two unbroken curves, for a married employee with two children and for a single man) with that ruling ten years later, in 1970 – the last year for which we

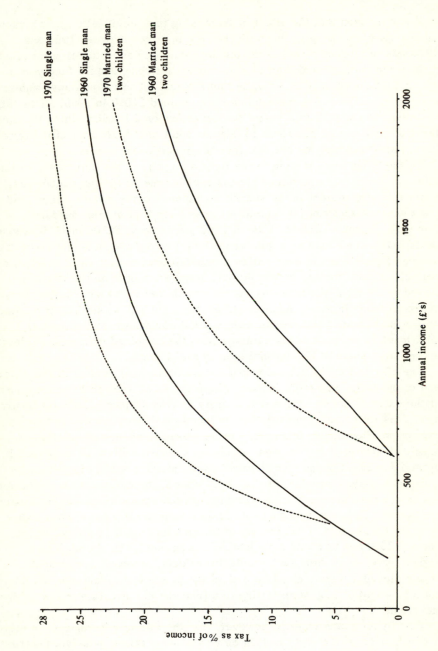

Graph II* Average rate of income tax on real earned incomes up to £2,000 (at 1960 prices), 1960 and 1970

have at writing reasonably complete information on incomes.[1] The equivalent 1970 curves are shown by hatched lines, and the two sets of curves represent the proportion of earnings deducted in tax from real incomes ranging up to £2000 p.a. in 1960, which is roughly equivalent to £3000 in cash for 1970.

It can be seen that the effect of increasing the individual's gross money income merely to keep in line with the rise in prices between 1960 and 1970 was to produce a rise in the proportionate burden of taxation for all single men earning more than £350 in the earlier year, and for family men who earned above £600 in 1960, so that *net* real income would have substantially declined. For the employee who earned £1000 in 1960, for instance, the effect of the shift to a higher tax curve involved in maintaining the same level of *gross* real income was to take an additional 5 per cent of the latter in tax, and to reduce his *net* real income proportionately more.

On the other hand, moving to the right along any of the curves shows the effect of an *increase* in earned pre-tax real income on the tax deductions, under the rates current in the year to which each curve relates. Thus, had the 1960 incidences of tax on real incomes been kept stable, our family man with the equivalent of £1000 at 1960 prices (say, £1500 in 1970) whose gross real income rose by a quarter in the following decade — not far off the average figure — would have suffered an additional deduction of nearly 5 per cent of his total income in tax. In fact, however, people on the whole both moved to the right along the tax curve, *and* shifted to a higher curve because of the increase in money incomes necessary merely to offset higher prices; so our unfortunate £1000-a-year man of 1960 would have lost almost an additional 10 per cent of his earnings from the combined movement — clearly a very large share of his nominal gain in real income.

The effect of specific government decisions is most evident at the lower end of the range of taxable income, where it will be seen that the steepness of the curve of tax deduction was sharply increased, particularly for family men. This reflected changes in the 'reduced rate' structure and in tax-exemption allowances. Otherwise the increased incidence of taxation at nearly all levels of income was largely an automatic effect of the general upward movement of incomes themselves — though it will be important for some later discussion that, as Graph II[*] shows, the curves of tax deduction are in any case steepest at the earnings level where workers begin to enter the tax net. Thus a single man with £500 a year in 1960 would have lost more than 5 per cent of his income to tax in adjusting it to prices, while one at £2000 a year would have lost only 3 per cent from the shift to a higher curve. Apart from such incidental effects, however, government action played a largely negative part in the process of heightened tax deduction — that of in general failing to adjust the tax structure to the incomes movement.

This by no means implies, however, that the role of governments in relation to the incidence of direct taxation on wages was entirely passive. Our first

(1) Data for 1971 or 1972 will, however, be given separately in this paper wherever possible and relevant.

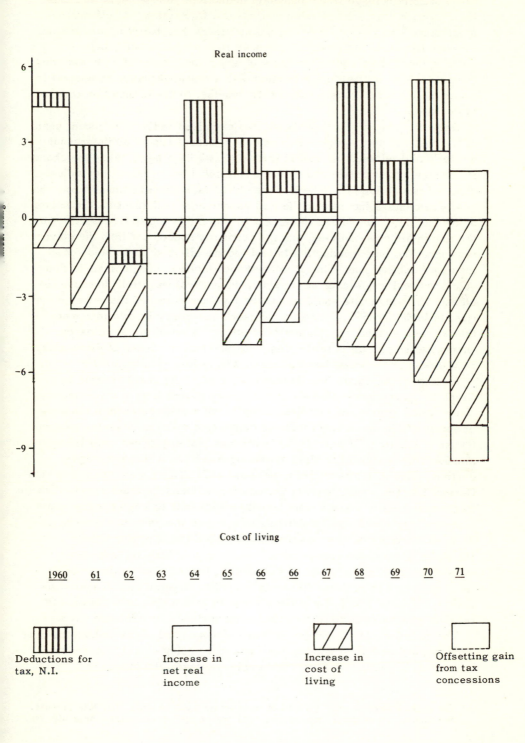

Graph III* Changes in median wage-earner's money income, living costs and tax deductions, 1959—1971

Real income

Cost of living

1960  61  62  63  64  65  66  66  67  68  69  70  71

Deductions for tax, N.I.

Increase in net real income

Increase in cost of living

Offsetting gain from tax concessions

73

Graph, indeed, perhaps conveys a misleading incidental impression of a fairly smooth increase in the burden of deductions from workers' incomes: there were, in fact, considerable year-to-year fluctuations. In effect, the progressive structure of these deductions meant that, *mutatis mutandis*, as incomes increased tax receipts rose more than proportionately both to incomes themselves and to the costs of any given volume of state services. Governments were therefore presented with a repeated choice of whether to retain the increased receipts (and then, whether to spend them), or whether to cut taxes.

Graph III[*] shows how this choice was exercised in the more recent years of the post-war period, again in terms of its annual impact on the manual worker's real retained income. In this Graph we have again taken the changes in the earnings and state deductions of a typical man wage-earner with a wife and two children.[1] The total height of each annual column shows that year's percentage increase in the median worker's cash income. The sector below the 'zero' line shows the extent to which this increase was offset by the rise in his cost-of-living, and the vertically-shaded cut from the column represents the further reduction in real income effected by tax and social insurance subtractions. Thus, the un-shaded block in each column is that year's net real wage-increase. In 1962, the net real wage fell, because increases in living costs and direct taxes together exceeded the money wage rise. In 1963 and 1971, the median worker's net money income rose more than wages, reduced taxation partially offsetting retail price increases. Otherwise the picture is fairly clear: the marginal incidence of direct taxes on wage-earners' income has fluctuated widely from year-to-year.

A complicating factor here is that over most of the years covered by Graph III[*] governments also attempted to apply some form of wage-restraint (later called 'prices and incomes policy'), and variations in their stance — or success — in this respect must be considered with the changing marginal burden of taxation. Thus, it is fairly obvious that employees' real living standards were allowed to rise, by relaxation either of taxes or wage-controls, more in 1959–60, 1963, 1970 and 1971. These were years in which General Elections were held, or immediately adjacent to those events. Governments have clearly taken a more permissive attitude to wage-earners' consumption just before and immediately after these watersheds. However, in between the years of what our first study called the 'Election Effect', increases in employee consumption have been held back by restraining wage-rises (and this in itself, if successful, limited also the increase in taxation, which is in Graph III[*] visibly smaller in years when wages rose little — 1962 and 1967). But if the attempt to hold wages back failed, tax receipts were allowed to rise instead — for instance, in 1961 and 1968.

The variations in the annual increase of wages and of tax deductions thus each display a cyclical pattern, the two cycles being closely interrelated and in turn dependent on a political cycle. However, the impact of a

---

(1) The median wage is used instead of the average here because that data permits us to carry the estimate forward into 1971 with some accuracy (see Appendix B).

progressive tax structure on rising incomes is such that the reductions in tax rates that governments make in their more relaxed phases have a necessarily ephemeral effect. Thus, the increase in net real income shown as arising from tax reductions in 1971 by Graph III* (or, for that matter, by the provisional figures of our Table 1*) in fact was concentrated in the first half of that year: in the second half the tax effect swung back into reverse. It can be roughly estimated that in April 1971 our typical wage-earner's weekly real disposable income had been increased by nearly 3 per cent over October 1970 as a result of the 1971 Budget's tax concessions. But in the following six months it was cut again by some 1½ per cent through tax deductions from his subsequent pay rises.

The 1971 Budget in fact represented a 'package' introduced by the new Conservative government to cut or redistribute both income taxes and social welfare benefits. The approximate total effect (again for married employees with two children) on men at different earnings levels is shown in Table 5*.

Table 5* *Changes (£ per annum) in taxes, social insurance contributions and social welfare benefits, April 1971, and subsequent effects of inflation*

| Workers at income level of: | Reduction in income tax | (Minus) Increase in graduated contribution | (Minus) Approximate reduction in social welfare benefits[a] | Net gain | Taxation on 'inflation proof' earnings increase to Oct. 1971[b] |
|---|---|---|---|---|---|
| Highest Decile | 58.2 | 34.0 | 20.5 | 3.7 | 22.5 |
| Upper Quartile | 51.0 | 19.4 | 20.5 | 11.1 | 22.8 |
| Median | 44.5 | 5.9 | 20.5 | 18.1 | 21.0 |
| Lower Quartile | 39.1 | 3.4 | 20.5 | 15.2 | 17.3 |
| Lowest Decile | 35.0 | 0.8 | 0.0 | 35.2 | 15.4 |

[a] Estimated loss from increased school meal and Health Service charges, abolition of free milk for schoolchildren and babies — except to workers below a minimum income figure (assuming they asked for free benefits).

[b] 'Inflation proof' earnings = money income required to provide constant net real income.

This Table, however, also shows the effect of increasing wages over the next six months to maintain the real value of these workers' disposable income in face of the price-inflation which actually occurred.[1] It will be seen that at every recorded level of wage-income, except the lowest, the subsequent 'automatic' increase in taxation would have exceeded the gain of the workers concerned from the April Budget.

Much the same effect will certainly follow the Conservative Government's second budget of 1972. In this, the Chancellor of the Exchequer introduced

(1) No comparable figures of earnings for later dates are as yet available, but this increase was certainly not far short of the actual one for this period.

a single major tax concession — an increase in the 'personal' exemption allowance of £135, a measure which was avowedly intended to put about £1 per week back into the average employee's pocket.[1] But one has only to assume (perhaps modestly in the context) an 8 per cent increase in wages from 1972 to 1973 for this gain to be more than eliminated by the resultant marginal increase in taxation.

It seems to be the fate of Labour Governments in Britain to tax employees more heavily (or restrain their real wages more effectively). Indeed, it almost appears — see Graph III* and Table 2* — as if the objective economic-historical role of the British Labour Party is to do (no doubt despite itself) those things to the workers that Conservative Governments are unable to do. However, the effect of our tax-structure/income-increase mechanism is clearly such as to give even Tory benevolence a transitory and self-cancelling character.

## Distributional effects of wage-taxation

The effects of taxation can be considered from several points of view, social and economic. A major argument for a progressive direct tax system (as opposed to other methods of taxation) is distributional: that it changes the allocation of income after tax in an egalitarian direction. It cannot, however, be held that this was the effect of the increasing British incidence of personal income taxation after the mid-1950's.

For instance, direct tax systems in general allow for the differing personal and family responsibilities of the taxpayers, and large families have in recent years been clearly identified as the major sufferers from poverty amongst income earners. Estimates of the rates of increase of net real income for various family units over the decade to 1970 are given in Table 6*. Here, we have assumed that the head of each unit received the national average weekly earnings for all men manual workers, that it received family allowance payments where appropriate, and that the appropriate tax exemption allowances were claimed. Since the same price index has been used to deflate each earnings series, differences in the rates of growth of net real income result from the combined effect of the changes in family allowance payments and of the differences in the incidence of tax between households of varying sizes.

It is clear that over the period 1960 to 1970 as a whole, the tendency has been for net real income to grow more slowly, the larger the family size. However, a consideration of the sub-periods reveals marked changes through the decade. Whereas it was the single man's net real income which grew at the slowest rate of the five groups between 1960 and 1964, during the second four years the tax effect was greatest for the married man with one child; and by 1969 to 1970 the three child family was suffering most. In the last two years the effect of tax was so severe on the income of the largest family

---

(1) Social insurance contributions were, however, increased to pay for increased benefits.

Table 6* *Rate of growth of real net income by family size*

| Compound annual increase % | Single person | Married man with wife and: | | | |
|---|---|---|---|---|---|
| | | No children | One child | Two children | Three children |
| 1960—64 | 0.94 | 1.04 | 1.33 | 1.28 | 1.30 |
| 1964—68 | 0.74 | 0.60 | 0.43 | 0.50 | 0.55 |
| 1968—70 | 2.13 | 2.08 | 1.79 | 1.29 | 0.90 |
| 1960—70 | 1.09 | 1.07 | 1.05 | 0.97 | 0.93 |

covered that its rate of increase of real disposable income was less than half that of the single man.

One reason for this somewhat curious effect is that the successive adjustments to tax-exemption allowances benefitted different degrees of personal responsibility to differing extents. It is, indeed, remarkable that over the whole post-war period these increases discriminated in favour of single people. Thus, the unmarried worker's personal allowance rose by 130 per cent from 1948 to 1970, that of the married taxpayer by 108 per cent, while the allowance for children under 11 years old was increased by only 91 per cent. Since, as we have said, these allowances *on the average* kept roughly in step with living costs, the effect was a real reduction of the living standards of families, which was not offset by the family allowance payments.[1] A second reason for the very marked discrimination shown in the last two years of Table 6*, particularly, was the steepened incidence of taxation on the incomes of family men just after their entry into the taxable income range, which has already been noted in connection with our Graph II*, and which was partly an effect of other changes in the tax structure between 1960 and 1970.

This steepening was, however, a fairly general effect, which involved the general distribution of net income between workers, as well as the particular aspect just discussed. It was observed previously in this paper (cf. Tables 2* and 3*) that on the whole men manual workers had suffered more heavily from an increasing marginal incidence of taxation than other employees. Table 7* shows how different levels of earning among manual workers themselves were affected by this trend.

At first sight this Table shows the effect one might expect from the theory of progressive taxation. Over the decade as a whole, net real earnings grew fastest at the lower decile, and the rate of increase falls off as we move across the distribution to a low point at the upper quartile. But after that point the rate of increase begins to recover; and consideration of the sub-periods shows that as the decade progressed the most serious erosion effected by tax increases to the growth of net real income was felt at lower and lower income levels. Thus, of the five income levels studied, the slowest growth of net real income moved from the highest decile level for 1960/64 to the median for 1968/70.

(1) These in any case applied only from the second child, and the only major increase in them (in 1968) was subject to a special tax which cancelled it for people in the tax-paying income range.

Table 7* *Rates of growth of net real earnings at different levels of manual worker earnings (married men with two children under 11 years old)*

| Compound annual increase % | Lowest decile | Lower quartile | Median | Upper quartile | Highest decile |
|---|---|---|---|---|---|
| 1960—64 | 2.01 | 1.80 | 1.45 | 1.28 | 1.16 |
| 1964—68 | 1.82 | 1.01 | 0.88 | 0.62 | 0.76 |
| 1968—70 | 2.52 | 1.88 | 1.49 | 1.64 | 1.93 |
| 1960—1970 | 2.04 | 1.51 | 1.23 | 1.09 | 1.17 |

Thus it seems that, as the 1960's progressed, tax began to bite more deeply into the earnings of lower-paid workers and workers with large family commitments. The previous Table, however, was compelled to assume that workers at different wage levels experienced the same percentage increase in earnings as the average over the years examined, because regular data on the actual distribution of earnings has only recently been collected. This is possibly not too unrealistic an assumption in the long run, during which it is known that the distribution of earnings has in the past tended to change little.[1] But it is not valid for shorter periods, and particularly for ones of sharp inflation, like that at the end of the 1960's. Table 8* shows

Table 8* *Changes (%) in money and real income at different earnings levels, Sept. 1968—April 1971*

| | Gross money income | Gross real income | Net real income |
|---|---|---|---|
| *Single man* | | | |
| Highest decile | 24.5 | 2.8 | 2.8 |
| Upper quartile | 25.2 | 3.4 | 2.6 |
| Median | 25.4 | 3.6 | 2.1 |
| Lower quartile | 26.4 | 4.4 | 2.8 |
| Lowest decile | 27.1 | 5.1 | 2.1 |
| *Married man, 2 children* | | | |
| Highest decile | 24.1 | 2.6 | 2.4 |
| Upper quartile | 24.7 | 3.1 | 2.2 |
| Median | 24.8 | 3.1 | 1.6 |
| Lower quartile | 25.7 | 3.8 | 2.9 |
| Lowest decile | 26.2 | 4.3 | 4.4 |

the actual income increase, together with the effects of increased prices and of tax deductions, at the different earnings levels reported by the New Earnings Survey first published for September 1968; it also combines our immediately preceding discussions by giving separate estimates for married and single men.

It will be seen that the general effect of wage increases over this two-and-a-half year period was to give a distinct preference to the lower-paid — partly a result of deliberate trade union policy (T.U.C. statements emphasised the achievement of a minimum earnings level as a major union objective): partly also, no doubt, in reflection of a common tendency of employers and

(1) Phelps Brown, E.H. and Browne, M.H., *Earnings in the Industries of the United Kingdom 1948—59*, *Economic Journal*, 1962.

arbitrators in times of severe inflation to concede bigger proportionate wage increases to those workers on whom increased prices are thought to bear most hardly. And since the percentage increase in living costs was assumed to be the same for workers at different earnings levels, this implied that the gross real income increase of the lowest-paid workers was almost twice that of the highest-paid group.

But this discrimination was almost entirely cancelled by the marginal effect of taxation. Indeed, workers at the highest level of earnings retained, on the whole, a larger increase in real terms than most other groups, and the smallest retained real advance was for the married man at a middling level of wages. The unmarried low-paid worker also did rather badly, and the lowest-paid family man was only permitted to retain his increase in gross real wages intact by the passing effect of the 1971 Budget's tax concessions, which removed him temporarily from the tax range.

In the case of manual workers, these various effects were a combined result of the movement of successively lower-paid cohorts of wage-earners into the tax-paying range, the differential real adjustments made to the various personal tax-exemption allowances, and (perhaps especially) the steepening of the marginal tax-rate at the point of entry into the tax net. However, it can equally be shown that the combined effect of income movements and changes in tax policy was to increase post-tax inequality between earned incomes in general. We noted in connection with our Graph II*that the increase in taxation for employees above the 1960 exemption limits was, up to 1970, smallest at the highest real gross income there depicted (£2000 p.a. in 1960, or £3000 in 1970). But the same progressive diminution of the marginal tax incidence extends to considerably higher earnings levels. Table 9* shows, again for the same decade up to 1970, the increase in the average tax rate involved in maintaining the same gross real income as in 1960 for different earnings groups, all of which are assumed to have risen sufficiently just to offset a 50 per cent rise in prices to 1970. (Here the calculation relates to single men, for simplicity's sake).

Table 9* *Increase in average tax rate at selected levels of real earned income*

| Real earnings p.a. at 1960 prices | £600 | £1000 | £2000 | £5000 | £20,000 |
|---|---|---|---|---|---|
| Increase in average tax rate, 1960—70 | 40% | 20% | 12% | −5% | 4% |

Thus in the comparatively modest income bracket of £900 to £1500 in 1970, the average tax rate had risen between two-fifths and one-fifth. At £7,500 earned income in 1970, the average tax rate had actually been reduced. This was largely a specific effect of a change in the surtax system in 1961, which (in the name of increasing 'incentive' to the productive middle classes) lifted the surtax exemption limits from £2000 to £5000 of income and reduced rates above this new level.

In general, however, the diminishing incidence of increased taxation on larger incomes arises because the effect of a general rise in incomes depends, for particular earnings brackets, on the relation between their marginal and average rates of tax. For higher-paid groups, the average tax rate is close to the marginal tax rate, so an increase in income will make little difference to the proportion of all income retained. But for people at the low end of the tax paying range, the average tax rate is small in relation to the marginal one; so here a rise in pay suffers a deduction which is disproportionately large relative to previous retained earnings. This relation between the average and marginal rates of tax at different income levels is thus critical to the impact of direct taxation and to tax policy.

We can note finally that if the increased incidence of tax deductions discriminated against lower-paid people and manual wage-earners, it also discriminated against employee income in general. We already have a calculation, unofficial, but from data supplied by the Treasury, of the proportions of corporate profits taken in taxation for dates between 1949 and 1968, and in Table 10* we have made, to parallel this series, a similar calculation of the proportion of total wages and salaries paid as tax. To company profits, the equivalent to the individual's tax allowances are capital tax exemption allowances of various kinds (including investment allowances) and these are an important factor in the trend of the profits columns.

Table 10* *The incidence of direct taxation on corporate income and employment incomes*

| Percentage of income taken as taxation from: | Corporate profits | | Wages and Salaries |
|---|---|---|---|
| | Excluding tax on dividends | Including tax on dividends | |
| 1949—1952 | 36.5 | 45.6 | 9.8 |
| 1953—1956 | 31.5 | 40.1 | 8.9 |
| 1957—1960 | 25.9 | 35.2 | 10.6 |
| 1961—1964 | 22.0 | 33.1 | 12.3 |
| 1965—1968 | 19.0 | 30.9 | 15.5 |

When we compare taxation on corporate income with taxation of wages and salaries, we find that between 1949—52 and 1953—56 the incidence of tax on both fell. After 1953—56, however, tax as a proportion of corporate income continued to fall whilst that on income from employment rose steadily. The share of corporate profits represented by taxation on dividends rose a little, but by only half as much as did taxes on employee earnings: and the increased tax yield on dividends was mainly due to larger distributions by companies.

How the opposite tendencies of taxation on profits and wages have affected relative shares in total income is suggested by Table 11*. Here total corporate profits are expressed as a ratio to aggregate wages and salaries. The calculation is made both before and after tax. Before tax the share of profits in total income fell between 1949—52 and 1965—68. After tax, however, the share of corporate income in the sum of profits and work-incomes increased from 20 per cent for 1949—52 to over 23 per cent in 1965—68, and the effect was to shift about 5 per cent of this sum from wages and salaries to corporate profits. Thus, before tax the distribution of factor income was changing in favour of wages and salaries and against company profits; but after tax this process was quite reversed.

Table 11* *Total corporate profits as a percentage of aggregate wages and salaries*

|  | Before tax | After tax[a] |
|---|---|---|
| 1949–52 | 41.6 | 25.0 |
| 1953–56 | 39.7 | 26.1 |
| 1957–60 | 39.5 | 28.7 |
| 1961–64 | 37.6 | 28.6 |
| 1965–68 | 37.2 | 30.2 |

[a]Including tax on dividends.

In this last respect it is notable that there is little difference between the effect of Conservative and Labour government tax policies; and some pressures which have borne upon Chancellors of the Exchequer in all sub-periods since the mid-1950's, and may themselves be in part a result of other tax effects, will be referred to later. Meanwhile we can note that from almost every point of view, the burden of direct taxation fell increasingly on lower incomes from work.

## Other effects: the balance of taxes and social benefits; investment and employment

Two other issues of tax policy are the relationship of direct taxes on income to indirect taxes on consumption, and the use of taxation to reallocate total expenditure in various ways — for instance, from private consumption to social benefits.

Table 12* *Proportions of indirect taxation in expenditure, and direct taxation in incomes*

|  | Taxes on expenditure as a percentage of consumer expenditure | Taxes on income as a percentage of: | |
|---|---|---|---|
|  |  | Total personal income | Total income from employment |
| 1961–64 | 17.1 | 15.0 | 11.2 |
| 1965–68 | 19.2 | 17.7 | 14.0 |
| 1969–70 | 20.9 | 19.7 | 16.4 |

It has been said that the general tendency of post-war British governments' fiscal policies was away from direct taxation, and towards indirect levies (purchase tax, etc.). This appears only to have been true, however, in the sense that direct taxes on corporate profits were reduced. The balance of taxes between *personal* income and *personal* consumption seems to have changed little during the period (the 1960's particularly) when income tax yields were increasing most sharply. Table 12* shows this effect. Table 12* shows again that increased income taxation bore most heavily on earnings from employment:[1] not only was the proportionate rise in tax deductions

(1) Total income from employment here includes H.M. Forces' pay and employers' contribution to National Insurance. However, there is very little difference in the proportionate increase of taxation for wages and salaries alone over this period.

sharpest on work incomes, but an additional 5.2 per cent of those incomes had been taken by direct taxes (between 1961/4 and the last date covered) compared with 4.7 per cent of personal income in general. However, the Table also shows that, over this period again, an additional 3 to 4 per cent of all consumers' expenditure was taken as taxes.

To what extent — if at all — this increased incidence of indirect taxation was (like a large part of the rise in income taxes) an automatic effect of rising expenditures, published data is insufficient to estimate. On the one hand, as real incomes increased (and they did slightly, even in the period of Table 12*) luxury spending would have risen more than proportionately, and such expenditure tends to be more highly taxed. On the other hand, much of British indirect taxation is raised as a flat-rate Excise Duty on alcohol and tobacco, and with inflation this type of taxation would (rates of levy being unchanged) show a declining relative proportion of all expenditure. However, in general increased taxation on consumption resulted from deliberate acts of government policy; so it also, of course, led to an average rise of retail prices. If we assume, very crudely, that the two foregoing effects cancelled out, so that (in the absence of changes in indirect tax rates) the total of such taxes would vary exactly pro-rata with changes in the total volume of consumer goods and services purchased, we can estimate very roughly what this rise in prices might have amounted to (Table 13*).

Table 13* *Approximate effect of expenditure taxes on prices*

| Annual average | Increase in indirect taxation contributing to price increases | Inflation of consumer expenditure resulting from price increases | Proportion of price increases resulting from increased indirect taxes |
|---|---|---|---|
| | £ million | £ million | % |
| 1960—1964 | 125 | 567 | 22.0 |
| 1964—1968 | 361 | 919 | 39.2 |
| 1968—1969 | 408 | 1534 | 26.6 |

Some care is needed in interpreting this table. Not only do the methods used to calculate the effect of indirect tax leave very much to be desired, but all Selective Employment Tax is included in the published official figures of indirect taxation, although SET was probably not all passed on to the consumer. On the other hand, our estimates are not completely out of line with others.[1] From Table 13* it seems at any rate clear that increased indirect taxation has itself contributed considerably to the inflation of prices. In effect, direct and indirect taxation acted in the 1960's as the two pincers of a trap. Increased consumption taxes put up prices, but to the extent that employees and others raised their incomes to cover their augmented living costs, direct taxation automatically took back a large part of the income increase — so much, indeed, that governments were able to make an occasional

(1) See National Institute of Economic and Social Research, *Economic Review*, February 1971, pp. 39. The NIESR estimated one third of the average increase in consumer prices 1967/8, and one half that for 1968/9, to be attributable to increased indirect taxation.

gracious demonstration of income tax reduction without substantially altering the balance of the two forms.

In general, therefore, the incidence of both types of taxation on personal income rose during the 1960's. But it is still possible that this increase represented a redistribution of growing real income from privately-directed consumption to social welfare provision.

Some analysis of the changing relative incidences of taxes and social benefits may be attempted, again, from official data, though the latter are also subject to serious reservations. For instance, the basic information is drawn from the Family Expenditure Survey, which is based on small samples, and is consequently liable to serious sampling errors; the response rate, although 70 per cent overall, is thought to be significantly lower for higher-income families and families with no children; and there is also an apparent under-reporting of expenditure on such items as alcoholic drinks and tobacco.

In this analysis, income before adjustment for taxes and benefits is called 'original income', and the definition of income in this usage is much broader than that used previously in this discussion. Estimates of payments in kind, imputed rent for owner-occupied houses and (following national accounting conventions) employers' contributions to social insurance funds, are all considered part of 'original income'. On the other hand (additionally to direct taxes on income and taxation on expenditure), employee social insurance contributions, local rates on accommodation, motor vehicle duties and radio and television licences are included as taxes. Benefits are those that can be easily allocated to individual households, such as family allowance payments, national insurance benefits, public welfare and health services, and education. But such provisions as defence, law and order and environmental services, which are not easily allocated, are excluded.

The upshot, however, at least indicates a trend. In Table 14[*] income adjusted for all taxes and benefits is shown as a percentage of original income

Table 14[*] *Income adjusted for taxes and benefits as a percentage of original income by household sizes*

| Size of household[a] | 1961—64 | 1965—68 | 1969—70 |
|---|---|---|---|
| 1 adult | 104 | 103 | 105 |
| 2 adults | 82 | 80 | 77 |
| 2 adults, 1 child | 81 | 78 | 76 |
| 2 adults, 2 children | 90 | 86 | 82 |
| 2 adults, 3 children | 101 | 96 | 93 |
| 2 adults, 4 children | 112 | 109 | 106 |
| All households in survey | 87 | 84 | 82 |

[a]Retired and non-retired households included

(so that if taxes and benefits for a particular household size just cancel out on average, adjusted income is shown in 100 per cent).

If we consider the calculation for all households together, it seems clear that the ratio of benefits-received to taxes-paid was falling during the 1960's. For particular household sizes, there was an increase in this ratio only for single adults (including widows and widowers), and then for 1969 alone: in that year changes in tax exemption allowances may have especially benefitted retired people. For all other groups, the household yield of benefits-received for taxes-paid fell steadily, and the fall was steepest for the conventionally typical family size — that of two adults with two children. And since the great majority of the households in the survey concerned are those of employees, it is virtually certain that the same falling trend of benefits to taxes was experienced by wage-earners.

Thus the increased taxation on employee incomes after the mid-1950's was far from being an egalitarian device: it certainly did not reflect a change from indirect to direct taxation; and it did not mainly arise from an increased distribution of social benefits.

In fact, of course, the dominating pressure on the policy of governments during this period — apart from those short-term electoral considerations to which we have already referred, and which surfaced intermittently, if with singularly disruptive effects — was the combined threat of balance of payments deficit and inflation. And to this, the response dictated by orthodox (or 'Treasury') doctrine was a restraint on total effective demand and consumption, plus a shift of the economic resources thus released to exports — and to productive investment as a means to long-term improvement in the national supply/demand equation and in international competiveness.

The restraint on consumption was certainly achieved, at least from the mid-1960's. Table 15* shows how the share of consumers' spending in total final expenditure fell. And the share of investment apparently rose, at least

Table 15* *Components of total final expenditure (at factor costs)*

| Percentage attributable to: | 1953—56 | 1957—60 | 1961—64 | 1965—68 | 1969—70 |
|---|---|---|---|---|---|
| Consumer expenditure | 52 | 53 | 52 | 50 | 48 |
| Public authority current expenditure | 15 | 14 | 15 | 16 | 16 |
| Gross domestic fixed capital formation (+ physical increase in stocks) | 13 | 15 | 16 | 17 | 16 |
| Exports, goods and services | 19 | 19 | 17 | 17 | 20 |

in the middle 1960's. But no improvement in the relative allocation of resources to exports was achieved until after the 1966—7 'freeze/severe restraint' on wage increases and the 1967 devaluation. Instead, there was an increase in the share of public authority current expenditures.

The instrument of the reduction in the consumers' share was a rapid growth in the central government's surplus on current account. The annual surplus increased from an average of some £440 million between 1961 and 1964 to £1,230 million between 1965 and 1968, and again to over £2,900 million in 1969. And although public investment rose (including that of local authorities, whose capital expenditure substantially depends on the central government), this by no means took up the balance. Thus, from 1961 to 1964, public authority savings were less than 70 per cent of their fixed investment; between 1965 and 1968 this ratio had increased to nearly 90 per cent and by 1969 it was 150 per cent. Perhaps the accumulating surplus was itself encouraging to a somewhat relaxed governmental attitude to its

growing current expenditure. But the increased share of investment is itself
somewhat deceptive. It is *industrial* investment which is most immediately
and directly associated with improvement in productivity and efficiency. The
great bulk of investment in new plant and machinery takes place in companies
and public corporations: Table 16* indicates the trend of this variety of
capital spending.

Table 16* *Shares of gross domestic fixed capital formation by sector (at market prices)*

| Percentage of total gross domestic fixed capital formation | 1953—56 | 1957—60 | 1961—64 | 1965—68 | 1969—70 |
|---|---|---|---|---|---|
| Personal | 17 | 16 | 16 | 14 | 13 |
| Companies and public corporations | 57 | 64 | 62 | 60 | 60 |
| Central government and local authorities | 26 | 20 | 22 | 26 | 27 |

In one major respect at least, therefore, the policy of restraining consumption was a failure: the share of directly productive investment declined
in the late 1960's. It seems possible that this failure of corporate investment
to take up the resources released from consumption was itself largely a consequence of the manner in which the restraint on consumption was achieved.
The increasing incidence of direct taxation on incomes (which were also
charges on production) meant that effective final demand was rising slower
than costs, so that pre-tax profits were squeezed — as we have already shown
in Table 11* — and the inducement to invest diminished. The growing government surplus led instead to increasing unemployment, which further clouded
the prospects for investment; and other consequences of the tax system's
working intensified the squeeze on profits. In effect, the device was also a
failure as an antidote to inflation: indeed, we shall argue that cost inflation
was not deterred by its operation but stimulated.

### Strikes and the stagnation of real net wages

We have suggested that the increasing incidence of direct taxation was an
important factor in augmenting unemployment (as, in a sense, it was meant
to be — though no doubt more so than governments intended). And it has also
been shown that increased taxation on consumption made a significant
direct contribution to rising prices: but this effect was itself intended to
release resources from consumption, to suppress demand inflation (again, in
effect) by creating unemployment. Why did these policies fail? We can perhaps
consider this question best in relation to the second problem from which this
study began. Why did the British strike-liability rise so sharply at the end of
the 1960's, despite increased and increasing unemployment?

The British strike-wave of 1969/71 had several features which are
peculiar by historical comparison. Historically, for instance, the annual
number (or frequency) of labour stoppages has tended to vary inversely to
the level of unemployment — presumably because workers are less willing

to risk a strike, and employers less willing to make concessions, when unemployment is high. Moreover, when unemployment is rising, the proportion
of all strikes which are in support of demands for wage increases is liable
to a special decline. But in the late 1960's in Britain, these relationships
were reversed — as Table 17* shows.

Table 17* *Unemployment and strikes in Great Britain (all industries except
mining and quarrying)*

| Annual average | Registered wholly unemployed (000's) | Total strikes | Wage increase strikes | Wage increase strikes as % of all strikes |
|---|---|---|---|---|
| 1961—64 | 402 | 1250 | 409 | 32.7 |
| 1965—68 | 420 | 1715 | 656 | 38.3 |
| 1969—70 | 539 | 3332 | 1846 | 55.2 |

The increase in the frequency of strikes, and of wage-increase strikes in
particular, coincides fairly clearly with the period of stagnating net real
wages of the late 1960's (cf. Graph III*). However, the interrelationship of
strike-frequency, unemployment and net real wages are traced somewhat
more closely in Graph IV* (which takes the series a little further back). It
will be seen that all three series show distinct cyclical fluctuations, but
that their inter-relationship is sharply changed about 1967. Up till that date,
the line for strikes moves in the opposite direction to that for unemployment,
while the curve for net real earnings tends to move in the same direction as
that for strikes. But in face of the stagnation of wage-earners' real income
which begins to be evident from 1965, the number of wage-increase strikes
rises sharply from 1966 to the end of the decade, despite the almost equally
sharp rise in unemployment, so that the previous inverse relation between
wage disputes and unemployment is completely disrupted.

This picture is itself perhaps sufficiently suggestive. However, the
frequency of strikes is not always a very reliable index of the level of
industrial unrest. In the previous table and in Graph IV*, for instance, we
excluded strikes in coal-mining (following a now well-established conven-
tion[1]) because in the 1950's this industry's high frequency of small
disputes dominated the series, but thereafter declined steeply, for reasons
probably specific to the industry itself. But this is not altogether a satisfactory procedure; and there are other reasons for not relying too much on
the reported frequency of disputes.[2]

Another, and statistically more reliable, indicator of labour unrest (though
it cannot necessarily be used for the same purposes) is the annual total of

(1) This device was first used, it is thought, by one of the writers (H.A. Turner,
*The Trend of Strikes*, Leeds University Press, 1963), to indicate that what then
seemed to him a certain widespread complacency as to the state of British
industrial relations was not altogether warranted. It has subsequently been used
in a variety of publications, official and unofficial, usually now to demonstrate
that matters are worse than he is inclined to think!

(2) Some of these are cited in H.A. Turner, *Is Britain Really Strike-Prone?* (D.A.E.
Occasional Paper, No. 20, C.U.P., 1969).

86

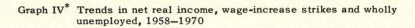

Graph IV* Trends in net real income, wage-increase strikes and wholly
unemployed, 1958—1970

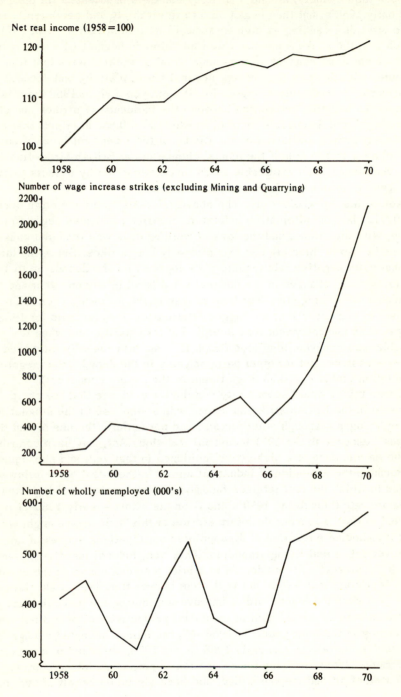

Net real income (1958=100)

Number of wage increase strikes (excluding Mining and Quarrying)

Number of wholly unemployed (000's)

working days reported as 'lost' from industrial disputes. This figure varied (though rather widely) around 3 million 'man-days of idleness' in the 1950's and early 1960's, but then began also to rise sharply and persistently from 1966 onwards (reaching as high as some 11 million striker-days in 1971, by which year the strike frequency itself had already begun to decline again).

If we correlate changes in the annual total of working days lost from disputes with those in the average net real wage, a strong and definite relationship immediately emerges. For the ten years up to 1969 there is a pronounced negative correlation between the incidence of strikes and changes in workers' real disposable income, in which $r^2 = 0.55$. In effect, this correlation (which is statistically significant at the 1 per cent level of confidence) says that over half the annual change in the British strike-liability over that decade was explicable as an inverse reaction by workers to current changes in the trend of their living standards.

Nor is this the whole story. The above relationship breaks down over 1970/71, when the alternative indicators of strike proneness began to point in opposite directions, and the loss of working days was rendered unusually severe by two or three big and exceptionally long strikes. But a similar emphatically negative relationship also appears, for the decade up to 1969 again, between changes in the net real wage level in any one year and the incidence of working days lost from strikes *in the following year*. This is subject to one exception: the lagged relationship does not hold for 1962/3 — a year when unemployment rose sharply but temporarily, and when real disposable earnings were also (see Graph III*, again) unusually increased by tax concessions. But for other pairs of years in the decade, this negative correlation yields $r^2 = 0.53$ (significant at the 2½ per cent level).

These things would seem pretty conclusive evidence that the sharp increase in the British strike-incidence was a response to the stagnation of net real wages — though other factors, and particularly the use of and the unions' response to the 1971 Industrial Relations Act, may have contributed to the maintenance of a high strike incidence in that year and subsequently.

Because the explosion of industrial unrest in the late 1960's followed a period in which the real retained incomes of wage-earners (having risen at a moderate rate through the 1950's and — on the whole — early 1960's) virtually ceased to rise, a reasonable interpretation of this strike wave might well be that it embodied a reaction of disappointed anticipations — ones of continuing improvement in real living standards. This was, indeed, just the explanation which the present writers adopted in a brief previous essay on the question:[1] 'The negligible increase in net real wage income from 1965, right through to 1969 (and even the higher rate of improvement during the preceding six years), contrasts with an annual gain in industrial productivity of over 3 per cent — increasing in the later years. In 1966—67, the unions accepted a wage-freeze and severe restraint. From early 1968 to mid-1970, so-called productivity agreements, often involving the relaxation of protective labour controls, or increased effort and responsibility, had been signed on behalf of over eight

(1) "Real Net Incomes and the Wage Explosion", *New Society*, loc. cit.

million workers. Overtime increased. The 1970 wage explosion may well represent, therefore, one of frustrated — but perhaps not altogether unjustified — expectations.'

There was in the chain of events undoubtedly a large element of legitimate expectation denied. But this aspect of the situation was to some extent specific to Britain, and to the history of relationships between the trade unions and the Labour Government of 1964—70: to concentrate only on the *general* level of net real earnings (as we have done above) is to neglect the *discriminatory* effects of inflation and a progressive tax system in combination, upon the living standards of different groups of employees and upon earnings differentials.

## Taxation, inflation and wage differentials

Table 18[*] analyses the increase in men's earnings in different industry groups over the five years immediately preceding the 'wage explosion' of 1970 and 1971.

Table 18[*] *Distribution of industry groups by annual compound rates of growth in weekly earnings of male manual workers (1964—69)*

| Annual compound rates of growth, percentage | No. of industry groups |
|---|---|
| Over 8.0 | 3 |
| 7.5—7.9 | 9 |
| 7.0—7.4 | 17 |
| 6.5—6.9 | 25 |
| 6.0—6.4 | 29 |
| 5.5—5.9 | 32 |
| 5.0—5.4 | 9 |
| Below 5.0 | 4 |

The average annual rate of growth of weekly earnings between 1964 and 1969 for all the 128 industry groups covered was 6.5 per cent compound. There was, however, a certain dispersal around this average. It will be seen, for instance, that in 45 groups average earnings increased by at least half a percentage point slower than the average annual rate of increase, and in 13 groups earnings rose at least 1 percentage point more slowly than the average rate. Over these years, the 6.5 per cent average rate of increase in gross money income produced an annual rise in net real income of 1.2 per cent per year for a single person or 0.7 per cent per year for a married man with two children. So that it is at once clear that many workers in the industry groups whose money earnings rose less than the mean must have experienced a negligible or negative improvement in net real income.

However, it is not sufficiently appreciated that the effect of inflation is in any case to amplify the impact on wage-relativities of what may superficially be quite small differences in the trend of earnings[1] — and that this

(1) For an internationally-comparative illustration, see Turner and Jackson. "On the Determination of the General Wage Level, etc.", *Economic Journal*, loc. cit., p. 834.

Table 19* *Illustration: differential effects of wage increases, inflation and taxation on wage relativities*

| | I | II | III | IV |
|---|---|---|---|---|
| (A) AMONG INDUSTRIES<br>Over five years: | In one-tenth of all industry groups, earnings rose by *less than:* | *On average,* earnings in all industries rose by: | In one-tenth of all industry groups, earnings rose by *more than:* | Relative spread of wage increases: $\left[\dfrac{\text{III}-\text{I}}{\text{II}}\right]$ |
| | % | % | % | |
| (1) Gross *money* wages | 31 | 37 | 44 | 0.35 |
| (2) Gross *real* wages | 6 | 10 | 16 | 0.99 |
| (3) *Net* money wages | 25 | 30 | 35 | 0.35 |
| (4) *Net real* wages | ½ | 5 | 9 | 1.63 |
| (B) BETWEEN 'EXTREME' GROUPS<br>(Gross *money* and gross *real* wages rise as in (1) and (2) above. *BUT:*) | *Low-paid/low rise* workers have increase of: | *Average* worker's increase: | *High-paid/high rise* workers have increase of: | Relative spread of wage increases: |
| | % | % | % | % |
| (5) *Net* money wages | 22 | 30 | 40 | 0.60 |
| (6) *Net real* wages | −1½ | 5 | 13 | 2.86 |

## NOTES ON ROWS

(1) The cumulative products of 5.5%, 6.5% and 7.5% annual increase for men manual workers over 1964 to 1969 (6.5% being the average for that period).

(2) Assuming the same consumers' price index applied to all groups; the average annual increase in prices being 4.4%.

(3) This indicates the effect of income tax on gross money wages with an *average* tax rate of approximately 15% and a *marginal* tax rate of approximately 30%, so that a gross increase of $x\%$ becomes a net increase, i.e. an increase in *disposable* income, of $\dfrac{x\% \times 0.70}{0.85}$.

(4) This indicates the combined effect of inflation and taxation, assuming inflation as in Note (2) and taxation as in Note (3).

(5) If wage increases are randomly distributed in relation to *initial* industry wage levels, then the 'high-rise' groups will include some workers with *high* initial wage levels, and the 'low-rise' groups will include some workers with *low* initial wage levels. Assuming that 'high wages' approximate to the ninth decile and 'low wages' to the first decile (£2,000 and £1,000 respectively and approximately in 1969) and that all workers have the same *marginal* tax rate of 30%, but that the *average* tax rate for the high paid is 25% and for the low paid is 5 per cent, then, by applying the formula shown in Note (3) above with the appropriate tax rates to the figures of row (1) we obtain row (5).

(6) Assuming inflation as in Note (2), applied to row (5).

amplification is further considerably increased when rising earnings are subject to a progressively 'stepped' marginal tax deduction. We do not have the kind of detailed statistics on retained earnings which would enable us to illustrate the point by direct factual data, but we can do so by a schematic illustration, coupling the information in Table 18* above with other estimates which can be taken as approximately valid for the period to which it relates. This is done in our *Illustration* (Table 19*) which starts by converting a selection of the previous Table's average growth rates of earnings to a cumulative increase in each case, and then applies to that result the rise in living costs and the estimated tax deduction over the five years concerned. (The detailed basis of the calculations is explained in the 'Notes on Rows').

The first part (A) of this *Illustration* shows the effect of a variation of one percentage point on either side of the annual overall average increase in men's earnings, on the assumption that all the industries concerned started from the *same* average earnings level. The last column (IV) measures the spread in their subsequent divergences of earnings by simply taking the difference between the highest and lowest increase in relation to the general average increase; and this is done in each row according to successive indicators of the movement of wages. Thus an increase of 31 per cent in gross money wages in the 'low-rise' group of industries ultimately emerges as an insignificant increase only (0.5 per cent) in net real wages, after allowing for price increases and taxation, whereas in the 'high-rise' group a gross cash wage increase of 44 per cent emerges as a real and disposable increase of 9 per cent. And in the process the divergence of wage movements between the two groups is very considerably increased.

What is remarkable about this process is that the effect of taxation is here neutral when this is considered simply as one on net *money* incomes (granted our assumption that in this case workers in all industries had approximately the same marginal tax rate): our measure of the relative 'spread' of wage increases (Col. IV) remains the same in both Row (1) and Row (3). But when combined with the effect of inflation, taxation substantially reinforces the former's discriminatory impact. The relative 'spread' of cash wage increases is trebled by the impact of rising prices alone: but it is multiplied fivefold in terms of *net* real wages. We can put the point here another way by saying that whereas over the five years covered by these calculations, workers in 'high-rise' industries had, on average, only a 40 per cent greater increase in nominal pay than those in 'low-rise' industries, their real wage increase was nearly three times greater, and their *net* real increase some seventeen times greater, than that of 'low rise' workers who started at the same earnings level.

These discriminatory effects, however, are still more sharply revealed by the second part (B) of the *Illustration*, which analyses the position of workers who started from *different* earnings levels (and thus from different average tax rates). Here we consider the trend of wages for those low-paid workers who happened to get wage-increases on the smaller side of the (to repeat) quite narrow range of annual percentage rises in gross pay, and we compare it with trends for 'high-paid/high-rise' workers. Percentagewise, these two extreme groups show no difference in their gross money and real wage increases from those experienced by other workers who had low or high wage-advances (respectively) but who started from the general average pay level. In terms of *net* money wages, however, taxation here somewhat widens the 'spread' of wage-increases independently (col. IV) over its original index of 0.35. But again, the impact of taxation and inflation *combined* is to widen the effective divergence of wage trends much more considerably. In this case, the 'spread' is multiplied eightfold from its initial nominal figure.

The point may perhaps be rubbed home by considering in absolute terms, rather than relative ones, the effects shown by our *Illustration's* second part upon the standards of the workers concerned. This is done in Table 20* (where the second row's figures are higher than the first's because net income in 1964 has been recalculated at its equivalent in 1969 prices).

Table 20* *Illustration: effects of wage increases, inflation and taxation on absolute wage differentials*

| £ | Low-paid/ low-rise industries | Average, all industries | High-paid/ high-rise industries |
|---|---|---|---|
| *1964 wage* | | | |
| Gross | 765 | 1095 | 1393 |
| Net *real* | 965 | 1215 | 1326 |
| (at 1969 prices) | | | |
| *Increase* *1964—69* | | | |
| Gross money | 235 | 405 | 607 |
| Gross *real* | 53 | 140 | 277 |
| *Net* real | −15 | 60 | 174 |
| *1969 wage* | | | |
| Net | 950 | 1275 | 1500 |
| Gross | 1000 | 1500 | 2000 |

*Source*: calculated from Table 19*.

This table shows, of course, how the cumulative effect of quite small differences in the percentage annual rate of gross wage increase may be to produce very large differences in the resultant additions to absolute nominal income. It also shows how what appears to be a quite large increase in the earnings of lower-paid workers may result in an actual decline in real income even when this is not implied by the rise in living costs alone. But it particularly shows that the widening in absolute differences in living standards may go (because again of the combined effect of inflation and taxation) much beyond that suggested by differences in the nominal rate of pay increase. Summarily:

*In gross money terms*:

the pay increase of 'high-paid/high-rise' workers is *1½ times* that of *'average'* workers;

93

the increase for 'average' workers is *twice* that for *'low-paid/low-rise'* workers.

*After allowing for price increases*:

the increase of 'high-paid/high-rise' workers is *twice* that for *'average'* workers; the increase of 'average' workers is *three times* that for *'low-paid/low-rise' workers*; and

*After allowing further for taxation*:

the increase for 'high-paid/high-rise' workers is *three times* that of *'average'* workers;
the real retained income of *'low-paid/low-rise'* workers has *fallen*.

Once again, therefore, we have a relationship in which a nominally progressive and 'levelling' direct tax system necessarily produces, in the presence of inflation, inegalitarian results.

It is thus clear that the negligible increase in net real wages from 1964 to 1969 concealed a situation in which some groups of workers were experiencing an actual decline in real living standards while others were enjoying a palpable improvement. Moreover, the calculations of our *Illustrations* neglect one further effect which was significant during the period to which they relate: they assume living costs rose at the same rate for all groups, whereas in fact there was apparently a slightly faster-than-average increase in the costs of low-income consumers.[1] It is possible that this is a normal effect of rapid inflation: since even under this circumstance prices of different commodities rise at different rates, consumers tend to switch their expenditure to goods which are thus becoming relatively cheaper, and those groups whose income is lagging behind are clearly under greater pressure to do so. On the other hand, their possibilities of switching may be less if they are also lowly-paid, since in their case a greater proportion of expenditure goes on necessities.

It must also be remembered that in our statistical analysis here we are still dealing with quite large industry groups. Unless, again, all workers within any such group have the same increase in earnings and start from the same initial wage-level, the same pattern of multiplying divergences in wage-trends would be repeated inside the groups themselves, so that for individual occupations or districts, and still more for individual workers, the range of actual experience would be considerably wider than that depicted in our *Illustrations*. The probability that significant numbers of 'low-paid/low-rise' workers had a perceptible fall in living standards over this period is thus considerably greater than these schematic calculations suggest.

There is clearly all the difference in the world between a situation where everybody's income is rising, but at slightly different rates (which is what the nominal, or even gross real earnings figures for the 1960's suggest), and

(1) See p. 67 above. Since the Index of Retail Prices has been put on a similar, "current weighting" basis to the alternative (but more comprehensive) C.S.O. index of prices of consumers' goods and services, it has tended to rise about 0.2 percentage points faster than the latter index each year.

one where some groups' living standards are being cut while relative differences in living standards are being widened. Certainly, in four major disputes of the 1970/71 and 1971/72 winters — those of the dustmen (local government sanitary employees), electricity power workers, and coal miners (who struck twice on a large scale) — it could be reasonably argued that not merely were living standards for these groups as a whole falling behind the external upward movement, but that important sections among their memberships had experienced a fall in net real income. *Relative* wage effects (which may not infrequently imply an absolute deterioration for some employees) may thus have been quite as important in the wage-explosion of 1970 and 1971 as the probable disappointment of established *average* expectations, and to these effects the system of taxation on wages made a major contribution.

**The tax-trap on wage moderation: militancy pays**

This analysis, however, raises one further problem. We are frequently told that large wage-demands cause increased prices, and are therefore self-cancelling: moreover, given an income tax system such as that which operated throughout the 1960's in Britain, the faster wages in general rise, the smaller the proportion of total wage income retained. To the extent that the wave of industrial militancy at the turn of the decade was designed to correct a perceived and previous wage-injustice, therefore, it could be argued to have been at least in some significant degree self-defeating.

There was, indeed, a certain hypocrisy in the suggestion, which was commonly attached during the 1960's to public sermons on the inflationary consequences of wage-claims, that workers should limit their wage demands to the equivalent of the annual rise in productivity. It can readily be shown that with a progressive tax system which reaches down to a large proportion of employees, with no change in tax rates or exemption allowances (which is almost always true for at least the year between Budgets), and with a successful policy by firms of raising price in proportion to any increase in unit costs, it is impossible for workers to raise their money wages sufficiently to secure such a predetermined increase in net real income.

This proposition can be illustrated by a numerical example, again. Suppose productivity is increasing at 2½ per cent per year (about the British normal rate for the economy as a whole). Suppose further that workers aim to secure just exactly that annual increase in net real income by raising money wages, having no initial knowledge of the tax system's effects and basing their expectation of price trends on what happened in their previous period of reference. Then the rates of increase in gross money, net money and net real wage-incomes, and in prices, are those set out in Table 21[*] (where we have assumed that all workers initially earn £30 per week, that the average wage is also for a man with a wife and two children, that tax rates and allowances are those current in the 1970/71 tax year and remain unchanged throughout, and that *initial* expectations are that prices will remain unchanged). In Year $T$ the workers aim for a 2.5 per cent increase in net real income, and in all innocence accept that this requires a gross money wage increase of the

Table 21* *Example: effects of 'moderate' wage-demands under normal*
*assumptions as to tax and price effects*[a]

| Percentage increase in: | Gross money wage | Net money income | Price increase | Net real income |
|---|---|---|---|---|
| $T$ | 2.5 | 2.1 | 0.0 | 2.1 |
| $T + 1$ | 3.4 | 2.9 | 0.9 | 2.0 |
| $T + 2$ | 5.0 | 4.3 | 2.5 | 1.8 |
| $T + 3$ | 7.8 | 6.6 | 5.3 | 1.3 |
| $T + 4$ | 12.3 | 10.6 | 9.8 | 0.8 |
| $T + 5$ | 19.1 | 16.8 | 16.6 | 0.2 |

[a]This calculation departs *very* slightly from strict mathematical accuracy, the figures being rounded off and produced arithmetically from line to line (or column to column), for ease of appreciation. However, a strict mathematical treatment would have still produced a net real income increase of only 0.50% in year $T + 5$!

same amount. But the tax deduction reduces this to 2.1 per cent. Having taken one taste of the Apple, in the second year, they claim sufficient — 3.4 per cent — to allow for this deduction and to recover their deficiency at the first round (thus aiming at 2.9 per cent net in all). But this money increase, being greater than the increase in productivity, raises unit costs by 0.9 per cent, so prices also increase by that amount. So real net income only rises 2.0 per cent. In the third year the workers make wage claims to raise real income by the increase in productivity to date, minus the 4.1 per cent net real income gain already secured. Adjusted for taxes and the second year's price increase, this amounts to a 5.0 per cent claim in money terms. However, *this* raises prices 2.5 per cent, so real net income only increases by 1.8 per cent. And so we go on, until the end of the period, at Year $T + 5$, money wages are rising at 19.1 per cent per year, prices at 16.8 per cent and net real income at only 0.2 per cent!

Under the fairly realistic assumptions of our *Example*, then, it would be impossible to increase money wages sufficiently to secure that net real wages rose in line with productivity, because where income taxes are progressive, gross wages must rise faster than net wages. *Gross* wages determine the rate of increase in industrial costs and hence in prices, and since gross wages must then increase faster than productivity, prices also rise. And when prices rise the real increase in net income is less than the money increase. We can vary the assumptions of this model to some extent (for instance, by assuming greater sophistication — or anticipation — in relation to the price increases expected by workers), but it will make no difference in principle to the result. Similarly, if we substitute a once-for-all autonomous increase in prices for the productivity increase, as being the figure for which workers initially aim to compensate themselves, the result is found to be a progressive reduction in living standards.

One would not, of course, suppose that workers (or even union leaders) were aware of the impossibility of 'beating the system' in quite such specific terms as those indicated by our *Example*. But the more general effects of wage-increases on prices and on marginal tax deductions were common currency. It was, indeed, frequently argued in 1970/71 that when other earnings-linked deductions or subsidies (such as those for some contributory employee pension schemes, or rent rebates on municipal housing) were taken into account, the marginal rate of deduction from many lower-paid workers' pay exceeded 100 per cent! Were workers suffering from a 'money illusion', which obscured their view of these essentials?

One answer to this question is of course that, while these things might possibly be true of wages *in general*, they were not necessarily true of the wages of particular groups of employees. As the analysis of our last section showed, and especially the *Illustrations* of Tables 19[*] and 20[*], in the late 1960's the effect of comparatively small differences in money wage-increases between such groups was to produce very big differences in the actual trend of their respective living standards. The impact of the tax system and inflation together was thus to induce a much intensified struggle for shares in the small addition to total real disposable wage-income which was available, in which less militant groups (or less successful ones – like the postmen, whose long national strike of winter 1970/1 ended in defeat) risked not merely a declining position in the relative wage-hierarchy but an actual fall in their standard of life, despite generally rising productivity.

However, this conflict over the *relative* distribution of net real income would hardly explain the attitude of the T.U.C. – which, as spokesman of labour interests in general, could only have found such a struggle divisive. It is indeed notable that while the T.U.C. rejected wage-restraint over the period from 1968 onwards, its pay-policy guidelines to its affiliated unions consistently emphasised a need to establish rising minimal standards for lower-paid workers. Moreover, the unions whose change of leadership and bargaining stance was most directly associated with the wave of labour militancy – the Transport and General Workers' Union and the Amalgamated Union of Engineering Workers – were themselves not just the two biggest (with nearly a third of all British trade union members between them), but also the most diverse in their membership and bargaining interests – the closest approximation to trade union 'conglomerates' – and the most involved in multiple negotiating arrangements embracing the interests of a great diversity of employees. Their particular militancy, therefore, could hardly be explained by a calculus of narrowly sectional gains.

The answer, apparently, is that it is not in fact true that, in wage-earners' actual recent experience, increases in pay have been self-cancelling, even beyond a certain level: on the contrary, such analysis as the recent data permits suggests that improvements in the living standards of workers in general have been fairly closely – but of course far from uniquely – related to the intensity of their pressure for money wage increases, and to the extent of their success in gaining them.

Thus if we again submit the period since 1959 to regression analysis, we find firstly that, if (as was previously indicated) years of stagnation or fall in the movement of net real earnings are ones of high strike-incidence, it is equally true that there is a direct relation between the annual incidence of strikes and the average annual increase of *gross money* wages. The correlation gives $r^2 = 0.33$ (so that the degree of labour militancy was clearly by no means the only factor in the annual rise of wages); but is nevertheless significant at the 2½ per cent level of confidence.

Secondly, it is certainly the case that the rate at which money wages rise is closely associated with the level of price-inflation. For the years 1959–71, again, there is a positive connection between the annual average wage and price increases which is measured by $r^2 = 0.47$ (significant at the 1 per cent level). The connection here is necessarily a two-way one, in which prices influence wages as well as vice-versa, but its detailed nature has been sufficiently explored (for our purposes) by other students.[1] For the moment, we can take it as given that the rate of price-inflation is at least considerably influenced by the pace at which money wages rise.

The important point, however, is that the effects of neither consequentially-increased prices nor consequentially-increased tax-deductions have been sufficient to offset — in the short run, at least — the gain from bigger wage-increases. Thus, if we consider (thirdly) the relationship between the annual rise in money wages over this period and that in gross real earnings, we find a positive correlation (significant at the 2½ per cent level) of $r^2 = 0.38$. The position (fourthly) in relation to *net* real wages is complicated by the fact that in certain years, reductions in income tax 'clawbacks' increased real disposable income more than would be implied by the money wage rise alone; but if we take these years (1960, 1963, and 1971) out of the comparison, a high positive correlation between the general rate of money wage increase and that of wage-earners' real disposable income emerges: $r^2 = 0.57$ (significant at the 1 per cent level). In the years there compared, moreover, the correlation between money wage movements and *gross* real wage increases, as well as its statistical significance, are both also sharply increased (to $r^2 = 0.87$ and 1 per cent respectively).[2]

These last two relationships are displayed in our Graph V*, which makes very clear the positive nature of the connection between general money wage-increases and workers' gains in either real wages or real disposable income. Which of these indicators is most relevant to the wage-earners' perception of the effects of labour militancy will depend to some extent on the income level from which they start and their personal family responsibilities — gross real wages being more meaningful to those still outside the tax net: but on either score, the evidence is, apparently, that militancy pays.

Indeed, the suggestion of Graph V* is that, *given the tax system, it is only by insisting on wage increases which are necessarily inflationary can wage-earners secure a 'moderate' gain in real living standards.* On the experience of 1960–70, to yield an increase of net real wages of 2½ per cent a year — approximately equivalent to the annual rise of productivity — required a money wage increase of over 8 per cent! On the other hand, a

(1) E.g., L.A. Dicks-Mireaux and J.C.R. Dow, 'The Determinants of Wage Inflation: United Kingdom, 1946–56' *Journal of the Royal Statistical Society*, Series A, (1959).

(2) The main reason for the improvement in the correlation is that the removal of 1971 takes out a year in which prices rose exceptionally fast in relation to wages (without 1971, the correlation is already improved from $r^2 = 0.38$ to $r^2 = 0.69$, significance 1 per cent). However, this rise may itself have been a delayed reaction to the very large wage increase of 1969/70.

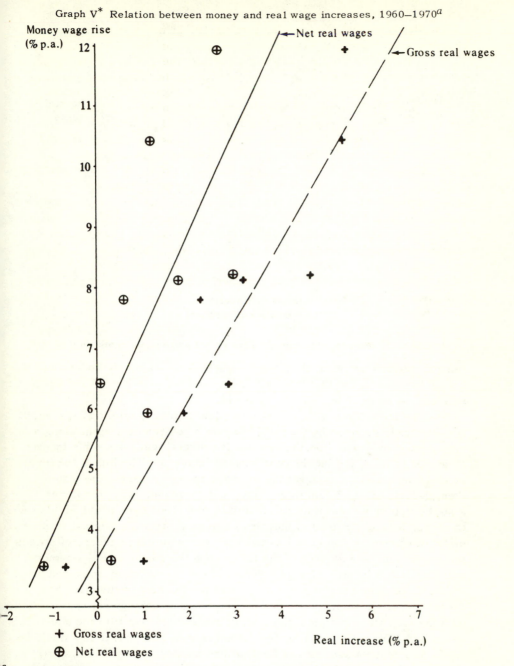

Graph V* Relation between money and real wage increases, 1960–1970[a]

Money wage rise (% p.a.)

← Net real wages

← Gross real wages

Real increase (% p.a.)

+ Gross real wages

⊕ Net real wages

[a]Excluding 1963

money wage rise of 3 to 4 per cent (which would have been barely acceptable as 'moderate' in terms of official incomes policies – Labour and Conservative – in the 1960's) tended to produce a nil change in gross real wages and an actual *fall* in net real wages. In the light of such experience, the remarkable

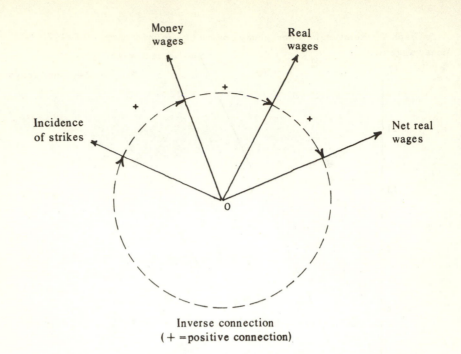

Graph VI[*] Inter-relationship of labour unrest and wage-earners' income

thing is perhaps not so much that governmental preaching of 'moderation' should be ignored, but that it should have received — in 1962/3 and again in 1966/7 — as much acceptance as it did.

What we are dealing with here is a cyclical series of relationships which may be simply depicted by Graph VI[*] (where a positive movement along a parameter is one away from the centre). If workers' real disposable income stagnates or falls, the incidence of strikes increases. The higher the level of strike-proneness, the bigger the increase in money wages: the faster, then, the rate at which real wages rise, and consequentially, the faster also the rise in net real wages. But this in turn feeds back to the incidence of strikes as a lower level of industrial unrest. So that the original *inverse* effect of changes in the growth of net real wages on the incidence of strikes returns as a *direct* influence of the latter upon the growth of wage-earners' real disposable income, through a series of effects on money wage and price inflation. One can conceive that a cyclical relationship of this kind may achieve a certain stability — a possibility which is perhaps not unconnected with the long stabilisation of the British strike-incidence from the mid-1930's to the mid-1950's. But equally, any disturbance of this equilibrium would be likely to produce a sequence of fluctuations running through the system. Which reinforces the statistical evidence that the cycles of increasing labour unrest from the mid-1950's on may be connected with that growing liability of labour incomes to state withholdings which our Tables 1[*] to 3[*] demonstrate as characteristic of that period. It is notable (see Graph VII[*], in our Appendix A) that the first general increase in the British strike liability coincided approximately with the introduction of the *average* wage-earner to the income-tax system's grasp, and that the more recent sharp increase in industrial conflict again approximately coincides with the date at which he became liable for the full rate of tax.

### A conclusion: wage-taxation, inflation, unemployment and labour unrest

There is, however, an evident inconsistency between the last conclusion, based on its immediately preceding statistical analysis of experience, that bigger wage-demands — or ones which are more determinedly-pressed — *do* produce a tangible gain in workers' real living standards, and our earlier conclusion (see the *Example* of Table 21[*]) that it was impossible, given a progressive direct tax system which included any large proportion of wage-earners in the tax net, for workers to pitch their wage-demands at a figure which would secure them any pre-determined increase in net real wages (such as a 'moderate' one).

The assumption of that *Example's* calculation, however, was that employers normally passed on increases in unit costs to prices. And the difference between what should hypothetically have occurred during the 1960's and what actually occurred was simply that, for a variety of reasons, employers were unable fully to do so. Of these reasons, however, perhaps the most important was that, largely because of the increase in nominal incomes, government tax receipts were increasing faster than planned government expenditure, and governments did not choose to either raise the latter or to cut taxes in full proportion. Or, to put the matter another (and the crudest possible) way, employers' costs were determined by the rise in *gross* money wages, but their demand was largely determined by the rise in *net* wages, which was smaller: and the government did not choose either to spend the difference itself or to abolish it.

To return to our hypothetical Table 21[*], again, over the six years of that calculation, productivity rises 16 per cent but net real income by only 8 per cent! Unless the difference is taken up by increased investment, exports, or public expenditure, there is excess capacity. And this, of course, is just what emerged. Employers could thus only increase prices in proportion to their increased unit costs by accepting a reduction in real demand, reducing output and creating unemployment. Some of them no doubt did so: but others preferred to accept a reduced rate of profit (witness, our Table 11[*]) — which permitted the increase in real wages to occur. But a decline in profitability was *equally* likely — either through direct reductions to future planned output or through restricted new investment — to produce increased unemployment. The cost to wage earners in general of a net real income increase which, even over the years covered in Graph V[*], amounted to little more than 1 per cent annually was thus a greatly reduced demand for labour itself.

We began this paper by referring to two problems — or rather, what were in the light of historical experience seeming contradictions — of contemporary industrial economies. One was the coincidence, at the end of the 1960's, of accelerated inflation with increased unemployment; the other was the parallel development of increased unemployment and much intensified labour militancy. And this study has been largely concerned with one factor which seems common to both phenomena: the effect of the entry of the mass of manual wage-earners, for the first time during peace, into the net of direct taxation. This was largely a result of the increase in wage-incomes themselves, but augmented government expenditures and general government economic policy also contributed to the movement. Because, however, in a progressive (and thus ostensibly equitable) tax-system, the marginal rate of tax on individual income is necessarily higher than the average rate, it was an inevitable consequence that bigger *gross* wage increases were required to maintain the accustomed rise of real *net* earnings — or even, for many groups, to prevent real living standards from falling. While the combined effect of inflation and increased wage-taxation was an increasing distortion of perceived differentials between wage-earners' living standards, so that many workers were also involved in attempts to restore their relative position.

The struggle of employees to achieve these things was far from fully successful, for reasons partly intrinsic to the process and partly arising from the fiscal beliefs of governments. But it contributed very substantially (to say the least) to both industrial unrest and inflation. Moreover, since the trend of effective demand was determined largely by *net* wage increases, while employers' costs were determined by *gross* wage increases, the growing gap between the two led to declining profitability and thus to increased unemployment.[1]

This study has been made from British data, but we suspect the situation with which it is concerned to be by no means unique to that country. It is certainly clear that some elements of the same interdependent mechanism have functioned in the U.S.A. For instance, consider the comparison in Table 22* (which covers the last decade for which data is currently available).

Table 22* *Wages, real disposable earnings, and strikes in the United States*

| % p.a. increase in: | Gross weekly earnings | Gross real earnings | Net real[a] earnings | Annual average working days lost from disputes (millions) |
|---|---|---|---|---|
| 1961/65 | 3.4 | 1.9 | 2.3 | 19.4 |
| 1966/70 | 4.7 | 0.8 | −0.3 | 45.2 |

[a]For wage-earner with three dependants.

It will be seen that there is the same tendency for workers' *net* real earnings to diverge from gross real wages, and to stagnate or fall in the late 1960's; and that this was accompanied by a similar sharp increase in the incidence

(1) Since this was written, Glyn and Sutcliffe (*British Capitalism, Workers and the Profits Squeeze*, Penguin, 1972) have attributed declining profitability to the pressure of wages against international competition. Our first study (and directly, *Economic Journal*, Dec. 1970, p. 846) suggests this effect also; but they have neglected both the taxation effects described here and the tax compensations to profits (see Table 11*), as well as the role of wage pressure in increased unemployment.

of strikes to that in the UK.[1] To which one might add, of course, that it was also accompanied by accelerated inflation and increased unemployment.

We are far from attributing the whole of the world acceleration in inflation at the end of the 1960's to the effects of taxation on wages. But that is not required: as our first study showed, it is only in the industrial capitalist countries that this acceleration has so far exceeded the upswing of the normal cyclical movement. And as that Paper also indicated, it is only necessary for such an acceleration to originate in one or two of the major industrial market economies for it to rapidly involve others.

But in any case, three things seem clear. One, that the relationship of wage-movements to those in prices, employment, living standards and social conflict cannot be adequately considered in conventional terms of money and real wages alone: the development and fluctuation of employee *real disposable* income has become a major third parameter which is of central importance to that relationship. Two, that those official fiscal policies which were, in the 1960's especially, most designed to restrain inflation may well in fact have been a major contributant to it — and in any case involved a quite unforeseen intensification of unemployment and industrial unrest. And three, that the effect of the generally-increased incidence of wage-taxation is to make the effective process of the determination of employee living standards almost as highly a politicised one as that we described in our first paper for the 'strato-inflationary' economies.

(1) Data for Australia, where there was also a substantial increase in the strike-incidence in the late 1960's, shows that the average rate of tax on employee earnings rose from 7 per cent in 1959/60, and 9 per cent in 1964/5, to 14 per cent in 1970/1.

# Appendix A
# Direct taxation on earned income

### Income tax

Under the British tax system, certain allowances are deducted from gross money income before taxes are levied. As far as income from employment is concerned, the most important of the tax allowances are: earned income allowance, personal allowance (which is higher for married than single persons), and children's allowance. Apart from these three, the only other tax allowance included in estimating the tax liability of different groups was one made against part of the employee national insurance and graduated contribution before 1965; in 1965 this allowance was abolished and compensated for by an increase in personal allowances. Together the allowances included in the analysis accounted for over 90 per cent of aggregate personal allowances and deductions for the tax years 1965/66 to 1968/69. [1] The other deductions allowable against tax on earned income include those for wife's earned income where working, housekeepers, dependent relatives, blind persons and life assurance premiums. These are excluded because they are not claimed by the majority of members of the groups covered by the partial analysis, and there is no way of calculating their average incidence with any certainty.

The changes in the basic allowances and rates of tax between the tax years 1948/49 and 1970/71 are shown in Table 23*.

### National insurance contributions

Flat rate insurance contributions are levied on all employees. In addition, since 1961, a graduated contribution has been paid. The changes in national insurance contributions between 1948 and 1972 are shown in Table 24* for workers not contracted out of the graduated pension scheme. Employees who are contracted out of this scheme pay a higher flate rate contribution and have, since 1966, been paying a reduced rate of graduated contributions.

### The combined effect

Graph VII* shows the year-by-year relationship, for a typical wage-earner, between earnings and the effective income-floor to direct taxation, from 1968 to 1971 (1972 earnings figures are not available at time of writing).

(1) *Inland Revenue Annual Report, 1971*, H.M. Stationery Office, Cmnd 4615, Table 30.

Graph VII*.  British wage income and tax levels

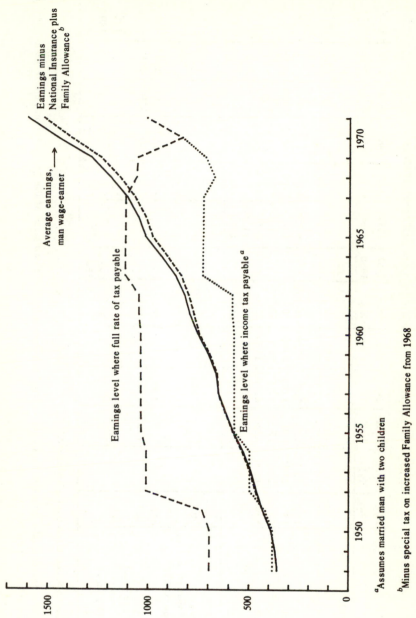

£ p.a.

Earnings minus
National Insurance plus
Family Allowance[b]

Average earnings,
man wage-earner

Earnings level where full rate of tax payable

Earnings level where income tax payable[a]

1500

1000

500

0

1950    1955    1960    1965    1970

[a]Assumes married man with two children

[b]Minus special tax on increased Family Allowance from 1968

Table 23* *New income tax rates and allowances 1948/49 to 1972/73*

| | 1948 1949 | 1950 1951 | 1951 1952 | 1952 1953 | 1953 1954 | 1955 1956 | 1957 1958 | 1959 1960 | 1963 1964 | 1965 1966 | 1969 1970 | 1970 1971 | 1971 1972 | 1972 1973 |
|---|---|---|---|---|---|---|---|---|---|---|---|---|---|---|
| **Rates of tax (%)** | | | | | | | | | | | | | | |
| Standard rate | 45% | | 47.5% | | 45% | 42.5% | | 38.75% | | 41.25% | | | 38.75% | |
| *Reduced rate* | | | | | | | | | | | | | | |
| Lowest rate | 15% | 12.5% | 15% | 15% | 12.5% | 11.25% | | 8.75% | 20% | | 30% | | | |
| Width of band | £50 | £50 | £50 | £100 | £100 | £60 | | £60 | £100 | | £260 | | | |
| Second rate | 30% | 25% | 27.5% | 27.5% | 25% | 23.75% | | 21.25% | 30% | | —[a] | —[a] | | |
| Width of band | £200 | £200 | £200 | £150 | £150 | £150 | | £150 | £200 | | —[a] | —[a] | | |
| Third rate | | | | 37.5% | 35% | 33.75% | | 31.25% | —[a] | | | | | |
| Width of band | | | | £150 | £150 | £150 | | £150 | —[a] | | | | | |
| **Tax allowances** | | | | | | | | | | | | | | |
| Earned income (percentage of earned income) | 20% | | | 22% | | | | | | | | | | |
| Personal (£s per year) | | | | | | | | | | | | | | |
| Single | 110 | | 190 | 120 | | 140 | | | 200 | 220[b] | 255 | 325 | | 460 |
| Married | 180 | | | 210 | | 240 | | | 320 | 340[b] | 375 | 465 | | 600 |
| Children[a] (£s per year) | | | | | | | | | | | | | | |
| 11 years and under | 60 | | 70 | 85 | | 100 | 125 | | 115 | | | | 155 | |
| 11 years to 16 years | | | " | " | | " | | | 140 | | | | 180 | |
| over 16 years | | | " | " | | " | 150 | | 165 | | | | 205 | |

[a] In these years reduced rates were eliminated.

[b] The increase in personal allowance in this year was to compensate for the elimination of the tax relief on part of the national insurance contribution paid by employees.

Table 24* *New national insurance contributions 1948 to 1972*[a]

| | 1948 | 1951 | 1952 | 1955 | 1957 | 1958 | 1961 | 1963 | 1965 | 1966 | 1968 | 1969 | 1971 | 1972 |
|---|---|---|---|---|---|---|---|---|---|---|---|---|---|---|
| **Flat rate contribution** (£s) per annum | 12.78 | 13.22 | 14.95 | 17.55 | 19.28 | 25.78 | 27.51 | 30.33 | 35.53 | | 43.33 | 45.93 | | |
| *Graduated contributions* | | | | | | | | | | | | | | |
| *First band* | | | | | | | | | | | | | | |
| Range of weekly earnings | | | | | | | | | | | | | | |
| From | | | | | | | £9 | £9 | | £9 | | | | |
| To | | | | | | | £15 | £18 | | £18 | | | | |
| Percentage paid as contribution | | | | | | | 4.25% | 4.25% | | 4.75% | | | | |
| *Second band* | | | | | | | | | | | | | | |
| From | | | | | | | | | | £18 | | £18 | £18 | £18 |
| To | | | | | | | | | | £30 | | £30 | £42 | £48 |
| Percentage paid as contribution | | | | | | | | | | 0.5% | | 3.25% | 4.35% | 4.75% |

[a] Rates for employees not contracted out of graduated pension scheme.

# Appendix B
# Methods, sources and notes

### Methods

For all calculations except those used in Table 3* and Graph Ib* the
method of adjusting income for direct tax was to assume a family size, add
family allowance to earned income, deduct basic tax allowances, calculate
the income tax on the remainder of income and then deduct income tax and
additional national insurance contributions from gross income to give net
income. Money incomes were adjusted to real values using the Index of
Retail Prices.

For Table 3* and Graph Ib*, aggregate wages and salaries before and
after adjustment for direct taxes were divided by numbers of employees in
employment to give gross and net money income per head. The deflator
used to adjust money incomes to real values was that published by the
CSO (Table 16, National Income and Expenditure, 1970).

For Graph II* the 1960 tax curve was constructed from estimates of income tax liability on annual earned incomes between £100 and £2,000
using 1960 tax rates and allowances. The 1970 tax curve results from a
similar exercise using 1970 tax rates and allowances on annual incomes
between £100 and £3,000: these income levels were then deflated by the
1970 Index of Retail Prices (1960–100). As the real value of both components of gross income – tax and disposable income – are affected to the
same extent by changing prices, the average rate of tax remains the same
whether real or money incomes are considered. By plotting the levels of income in the deflated series against the percentage of income paid in tax
in 1970 on corresponding levels of money income, a comparison can be
made between rates of tax in 1960 and 1970 on given levels of real income.

### Other tables and graphs

*Tables 1*, 2* and 6*, Graph Ia*

*Sources*: Department of Employment (DE), October Earnings Enquiry,
*Department of Employment Gazette.*

*Table 3* and Graph Ib*

*Sources*: CSO, *National Income and Expenditure*, HMSO, e.g. 1970, Tables
19 and 47. Department of Employment, *British Labour Statistics, Historical
Abstract, 1886–1968*, HMSO 1971, Table 132, and CSO, *Annual Abstract of
Statistics*, HMSO, 1970, Table 131, for 1969 figure

*Tables 4\*, 7\*, Graph III\**

*Sources*: *New Earnings Survey, 1970 and 1971,* Department of Employment, HMSO, 1971, *and D E Gazette.*

*Method*: Average earnings figure at each level of income for 1970 was calculated by working forward from the April New Earning Enquiry to October 1970 by using the DE monthly earning enquiry and averaging the April and October figures. Estimates for 1969 were obtained by working back from the 1970 average earnings, again using the monthly earning enquiry index. From 1959 to 1969 annual average earnings were calculated using an index based on the DE April and October Earnings Enquiry.

*Tables 5\* and 8\**

*Sources*: *New Earnings Survey,* September 1968 and April 1971, *DE Gazette*

*Table 9\**

*Source*: Inland Revenue Annual Reports HMSO 1960 and 1970.

*Note*: Between 1960 and 1970 prices increased by approximately 50 per cent. Consequently, the maintenance of the 1960 levels of real income required 50 per cent more income in money terms by 1970. By using amounts and average rates of income tax and surtax on 'specimen' incomes published in the Inland Revenue Annual Report for 1960 and 1970 it is possible to show the change in taxation on certain levels of real income. For example, the average rate of tax on £900 in 1970 is compared with that on £600 pounds in 1960.

*Tables 10\* and 11\**

*Sources*: Taxes on Corporate Income: *Trade Union Congress 'Economic Review',* 1970, p. 65. Taxes on Wages and Salaries: CSO, *National Income and Expenditure,* HMSO.

*Tables 12\*, 13\*, 15\*, 16\**

*Source*: CSO, *National Income and Expenditure,* HMSO.

*Table 14\**

*Source*: CSO, *Economic Trends,* HMSO, p. xxxv, Table 5, February 1971.

*Tables 17\* and 18\**

*Source*: *DE Gazette.*

*Tables 19\*, 20\* and 21\**

*Source*: Authors' calculations.

*Table 22\**

*Sources*: Government Printing Office, Washington, *Economic Report of the President to Congress,* January, 1972. U.S. Department of Labor, *Monthly Labor Review.*

*Graphs IV\*, V\* and VI\**

*Source*: Authors' calculations, *DE Gazette*.

*Graph VII\**, Tables 23\* and 24\*

*Source*: As stated in Appendix A.

# 4. Summary points - and policy conclusion

*(H.A. Turner)*

Each of the two preceding studies has its own summary, which it seems unnecessary to recapitulate lengthily here. Of the first study, the central suggestion is that a persistent pressure to inflation is, not a remediable defect, but an integral quality of the contemporary national economy and of international trade. In a very large sense — and this the study holds valid for modern economies of virtually all types — developments in the economic role of the state and in autonomous socio-economic organisation have converted Lord Robbins' theoretical dictum of the 1930's, that economics is the science of scarce means and unlimited ends, [1] into an operative reality. But the rate of inflation which follows from that condition, and the degree of instability which it involves, are closely bound up with the level of social and industrial conflict in particular societies, and depend on mechanisms which are not merely economic but also highly social and political in character.

Our second study's more restricted but more detailed survey links with the first in several ways. The immense growth of the state's economic importance is here reflected in the increased incidence of taxation on wages, and the significance of autonomous socio-economic organisation in the recent labour and union reaction to that increase, however perceived. Its major points are twofold (and though they are made for British experience, they must at least, if the Study's Table 22* has any meaning, be also substantially true of the United States). One, that the sharp rise in inflationary wage-pressure and industrial unrest (as well, probably in unemployment) that terminated the 1960's were significantly connected with the almost automatically increasing impact on wages of progressive tax-deductions. Two — perhaps more important in the longer run — that the effective rate of increase of employee living standards depends much more on government decision than on the success of union wage demands and the movements of nominal money wages or of prices.

But both studies overlap in noting the large relevance of social conflict to economic events. Non-Marxist economists, with few exceptions, [2] have

---

(1) In *An Essay on the Nature and Significance of Economic Science* (Macmillan, 1932), p. 15.

(2) Pen *Harmony and Conflict in Modern Society*, *op. cit.*, and in a more abstract way, Kenneth Boulding *Conflict and Defense: A General Theory* (Harper, New York, 1962) are noteworthy.

largely ignored the importance of social conflict and adjustment in economic processes: but to the mechanics of inflation these things appear vital.

Having said that, we can perhaps look briefly again at the question which provoked the present assembly of data, propositions and argument — if the question has not been partially answered incidentally to the exposition itself. Do *trade unions* cause inflation? These studies indicate several ways in which unions may, and often do, help to promote or perpetuate it. Workers' demands and expectations are an important part of the intrinsic and universal pressure for 'More!' that drives the contemporary economy, and unions help to focus and transmit those claims upon it. Granted that this pressure exists, moreover, our Introduction indicated at least three ways in which unions tend to make whatever level of inflation results compatible only with a lower level of employment than might exist in their absence. They sometimes impose restrictions on entry into jobs or occupations which should expand, and other restraints on labour mobility. Collective bargaining and formal wage-negotiation in themselves mean that organised workers will tend to get wage increases at a higher level of unemployment than would otherwise be the case. And the wage-fixing institutions which generally accompany union growth have the same general result. Moreover (one could add), if total employment is reduced by these effects, the extra unemployment may itself be a subject of union political pressure and agitation.

Our first study also suggests that unions may, and commonly do, form a significant part of the mechanisms it describes. They participate in 'equilibrium' inflations in two ways. The relationship between wages and high productivity growth in the 'key' sectors reconciles, we suggested, the reluctance of monopolistic or oligopolistic enterprises to reduce prices with the employee interest in higher pay, and unions focus and formalise that interest. While unions again commonly act as channels through which the 'high-productivity' wage-increase is conveyed to the economy at large. Unions are also actors and instruments in the social conflicts which may push an economy into strato-inflation, and which tend to make the latter process both irreversible and violently unstable. And unions have also acted (quite consciously, in several British instances at least [1]) as agents of that response to increased wage-taxation which our second study indicated as an important contributor to the recent upsurge of labour unrest and inflation in industrial market countries.

So unions *do* contribute to inflationary processes, and it is reasonable to suppose that differing national degrees of union organisational strength and militancy will make *some* difference to the character and intensity of those processes. But in most of the above circumstances, and without a conscious,

---

(1) Cf., for instance, "A Positive Employment Programme for I.C.I.: wage claim submitted to the Imperial Chemical Industries, Ltd., by the I.C.I. Signatory Unions" (Printed and distributed by the T. & G.W.U.), or "A Special Case? Social Justice and the Miners" (Edited for the N.U.M. by J. Hughes and R. Moore, Penguin, 1972).

concerted and collective attempt to re-arrange matters, it is hard to see how things could fall out differently. It is natural that workers should want high employment and employment security, increased social expenditure and direct pay improvements: that is why, in general, they join unions. If the unions are not there, the pressure on the economy often finds other channels (like those of politics). Since unions exist to improve their members' living standards, it also seems inevitable that their existence should make some impact on the employment/wage increase relationship; but other wage-fixing institutions, which also achieve that effect, have often been created in an attempt by governments or employers to anticipate or inhibit union growth.

Where the mechanics of inflation are concerned, moreover, it would be extraordinary for unions to deny their members wage-increases if employers are prepared to concede them without resistance: what we called the 'key' sectors are not always highly-unionised, and we noted that pay in them may rise as much by autonomous managerial decision or by 'wage drift' as by formal negotiation. And if that happens, it would not merely be usually impracticable for unions else-where to go against their members' demands for equitably comparable increases, but on the whole economically wrong for them to do so. To allow a differential between workers with comparable skills, responsibilities and conditions in different sectors of the economy to become permanently established and persistently widen would introduce increasing distortions in the allocation of labour and other resources between different productive uses. And it is clearly very possible that if unions had not focussed the employee reaction to increased taxation, it would have emerged in other ways — a spread of tax evasion devices, of compensations of a sort already familiar at higher salary levels, and so on: in the light of our second study, indeed, wage-earners' perceptions appear to be less blurred by a 'money illusion' than have been those of labour economists.

Moreover, it should by now be *very* clear, not merely that unions are far from being the only significant factor in the inflationary situation, but that they are not generally an independent factor in it. Our two studies emphasise the reaction of social organisations to their economic context, and their interaction with the latter. Internationally, there seems in fact no very obvious correspondence between rates and patterns of inflation and national differences in union strength and militancy, so if — as we inferred — union postures have some influence, it must in general be overwhelmed by other, pressures. In the strato-inflationary economies, for instance, unions are generally weaker than in the industrial countries which have experienced mere equilibrium inflation. It is not possible, in other words, to consider unions' responsibilities for inflation apart from their involvement and interaction with other parties to its mechanics.

One short answer to this Paper's title question, therefore, might be: in the modern economy, almost everybody 'causes' inflation. What *does* seem to emerge from these discussions, however, is that, where unions are both important and independent of the state, it is increasingly difficult to control inflation, and impossible to cure it, without a viable and broad union agreement to the appropriate measures. It is at this point that the attitudes of unions appear to us to become most significant: in some national union movements, for example, and in some individual unions elsewhere, attitudes to any co-operation of this kind are obviously so hostile as to make its possibility highly uncertain.

But even union attitudes are not fixed and determined in isolation, independently of the policies and attitudes of other major participants in the social economy. And what the studies perhaps emphasise most is the role — above that of unions, interest associations or firms — of governments in relation to rising prices. To repeat, a persisting pressure to inflation appears in the nature of the modern economy itself, whether communist, industrial capitalist, or developing. But the extent to which that pressure becomes economically or socially destructive depends on the political capacity of governments to achieve consensus or acquiescence in the multiple measures necessary for its confinement, and to deny themselves important short-run advantages which will otherwise later aggravate it.

Which introduces this study's policy implications. But before discussing them, we should perhaps revisit one feature that perhaps makes their consideration rather more urgent. That is that the forces which have hitherto kept most non-communist economies to an approximate 'equilibrium' path are weakening. In leading industrial capitalist economies, the disturbance provoked by the entry of the mass of the manual working-class into the reach of progressive income tax systems is, from the nature of the effect, an incipiently recurrent one. Our first study noted a recent relaxation of the international restraints on departures from equilibrium inflation. And perversely, the development and wide-spread adoption — if only intermittently — of governmental 'wage restraints', 'national wage policies' or 'incomes policies' as an anti-inflationary device since World War II, has in one sense actually contributed to the risk that equilibrium inflations will become strato-inflations (notwithstanding that such policies are implicitly recommended by this Paper's Introduction). The incidental result of this particular development in state policies has been to bring formal wage-determination into politics. The 'political cycle' (as our second study called it), determined by the electoral calculi of governments and political parties, which had previously been restricted to such things as the alternation of severity and indulgence in taxation, was thus extended to the government's influence on wage-fixing. And successive bouts of restraint and relaxation may well — as the British case suggests, again — risk destabilizing the inflationary 'equilibrium' to a degree from which it is hard to recover.

A point on which these studies have not dwelt, however, is that the impact, on union wage-policy and on price-fixing by firms, of government-engineered restrictions on demand and employment is also visibly declining. Firms and unions, fairly clearly, have learnt that governments cannot afford to allow recessions to go too deep or last too long; unemployment and excess capacity are increasingly (and on the whole correctly) attributed by industry to government policies rather than to its own price and wage decisions, and the latter become increasingly inflexible to depressed demand.

Thus, experience has also taught the major groups of organised workers that recessions of the post-war depth have little impact on their sectional bargaining power, if only because such recessions' most pronounced effect is an expulsion or withdrawal from the labour market of (less-organised) 'secondary workers' — married women, people of retiring age, adolescents, foreigners, and so on.[1] Indeed, it is even possible that just as oligopolistic business has sometimes argued (the British automobile industry is outstanding here) that when production is slack higher fixed costs per unit make price increases more necessary, so the pressure on the living standards of the relatively well-organised 'primary workers' may increase in time of recession. The 'secondary labour' which loses its jobs is partly made up of the primary workers' wives and families: and diminished family income may even be a force increasing the pressure behind union demands at such times.

Moreover, even for well-entrenched business or unions, recessions bear unevenly. *Some* fall behind, in profit or wage rates, in the recessionary episodes; and their attempt to recover their position on the upswing may set off a 'whipsaw' movement of price-price or wage-wage spirals which risks de-stabilising the normal inflationary process. Firms or unions whose long-run prospect of maintaining their relative earnings position is poor may now be particularly agressive in times which appear to them relatively favourable, because they fear the opportunity to offset future loss by present gain may not recur. So the three major British strikes in 1972 to time of writing (which have already pushed the annual British incidence of labour unrest up to a figure unrivalled since the General Strike year of 1926, and which clearly dislocated the Conservative government's general intentions for wage-move-ments and labour relations) were all in industries where employment was de-clining steeply: the mines, railways and docks. At any rate, in association with those other recent relaxations of the constraints towards equilibrium inflation to which we have already referred, these things perhaps make it more likely that individual countries may be pushed over the critical boundary into strato-inflation.

Some of the policy conclusions that follow from this Paper's analyses are negative, but nevertheless important. For instance, our second study indicates (fairly decisively, one might think) that 'orthodox' fiscal policy against infla-tion, which as it was practised in Britain in the 1960's was conceived as mopping up excess demand by increasing taxation — or, even more, by allowing direct tax receipts to rise disproportionately to income — had in fact a perverse effect. Increases in indirect taxation (of several kinds) raised prices and increased the pressure behind wage-demands: and that was par-ticularly the impact of the increasing marginal rate of deduction, by income tax and other levies, from wage-income. In effect, this tax policy was an implicit breach of the social and industrial conventions on which the

(1) For an early but statistically and analytically detailed illustration of this effect, see Turner "Employment Fluctuations, Labour Supply and Bargaining Power", *The Manchester School*, May 1959.

preservation of a merely equilibrium rate of inflation depended, and provoked a proportionately violent social and industrial reaction.

Equally, these analyses warn against simple nostrums. If inflation, as our first study suggests, both is intrinsic to the contemporary economy and involves necessarily a complex of major social mechanisms and interactions, it would be naive in the extreme to hope that it can be cured or controlled by some single device or prescription which affects only one element in or partner to the inflationary process. Rather, an armoury of methods and approaches — some of which are necessarily still experimental — is required to operate in combination.

For instance, increasing the rate of productivity growth is not a cure-all for inflation. Obviously, it is helpful to a government subject to many ambitions, demands and pressures to have more resources at its disposal: and to that extent, an acceleration of productivity growth would create better conditions within which measures to control rising prices could operate. But both our Introduction and the detailed analysis of our second study indicate, in different ways, that for most economies a rise in the rate of productivity growth would, of itself, tend to produce at least a parallel acceleration in the average rate of wage-increase. There are even good empirical reasons to think that, in some industrial countries at least, detailed wage-arrangements make such a productivity boost likely, other things being equal, actually to accentuate wage-inflation.[1]

Similarly, the sundry suggestions that wage-increases which were defined as 'excessive' should be subject to an extra tax is not hopeful. Improvements in tax arrangements would be, as our second study (and later, this Conclusion indicate, an important measure to limit inflation. But if a deliberately penal tax of the variety now quite widely proposed bore mainly on employers, they would pass at least part of it on to prices, and this would increase wage-pressure, not reduce it. And the same result would certainly follow if the tax were levied directly on wages: in several countries, at least, we already effectively have such a tax, which produces just that consequence.

Or again, legislation which is aimed selectively at one partner to the inflationary process alone, to 'correct trade union monopoly' or 'restore the balance of bargaining' is not likely to be productive. In pluralistic societies, a high degree of consensus, co-operation or at least acquiescence by major social groups is essential if measures to control inflation are to succeed. As both our first and second studies show, an intensification in social conflict leads directly to an accelerated inflation. An appropriate incomes policy requires an appropriate industrial relations policy (indeed, it is arguably a major error of both the recent Labour and the current Conservative governments in Britain that they have, in practice, considered industrial relations policy and incomes policy as alternative regulatory devices, not as complementaries

(1) Cf. Turner, "Employment Fluctuations, Cost-Inflation and Productivity in Manufacturing Industry", *International Labour Review*, May 1960, and (particularly on the Dutch experience) Turner and Jackson, "On the Stability of Wage Differences, etc." *British Journal of Industrial Relations*, loc. cit.

which need to be considered from that view-point). And inflation control equally requires an appropriate policy towards, for instance, oligopolistic price-determination and monopolies. But selective or discriminatory measures which intensify social conflict are to be avoided — at least, if inflation control is a major objective of policy.

One could go on to consider, for example, the proposition — which some still maintain — that all that is necessary to cure inflation is to appropriately restrict overall demand, employment and economic activity by monetary/fiscal measures. But that view has perhaps been sufficiently damaged already by recent economic events in the industrial market economies (which is not to say that overall demand management is not a central anti-inflationary requisite). So perhaps we should look rather at this Paper's more positive policy implications.

We will not discuss here the kind of measures which might help the 'strato-inflationary' economies to overcome that condition. Some could be suggested,[1] but there seems also substance in the argument that only a fundamental economic and social reconstruction could change their situation. Strato-inflation is clearly not necessarily incompatible with economic growth and comparative prosperity: it is certainly incompatible with social and political equity or stability; so the argument for such a reconstruction is not to be considered in relation to the inflation rate alone. For most countries, however, the important conclusion from our second study's discussion of these economies is that it is now risky in the extreme to allow the annual inflation rate to rise as high as 10 per cent: the acceleration may prove irreversible. [2]

But for the general run of 'capitalist', 'industrial market', 'mixed', 'developing' or 'underdeveloped' economies (titles this time according to taste), it might well be held that to suppress inflation absolutely would be a task demanding altogether too much political control, economic regulation and social integration. In that case, the problem could rather be put as one of how to keep inflation to the 'equilibrium' rate — towards which our first study indicated powerful and continuing centripetal pressures — and to avoid the kind of shocks and fluctuations that might push the society into aggravated social and industrial conflict, if not into strato-inflation itself. This implies that the equilibrium rate is intrinsically tolerable: but the attitude must also reckon with the possibly increasing difficulty of maintaining it.

(1) See, for instance, p. 39 n. 2.

(2) We say this notwithstanding that the world inflation rate did in fact exceed that figure in 1951. The circumstances then were somewhat special: in several countries, wage and price controls established in the Second World War were still in operation, and these were re-imposed in the United States. To the extent that the Korean War price-inflation was mixed with the effects of the preceding devaluations (e.g. by Britain) these were really a world revaluation of the dollar, rather than isolated national adjustments of the subsequent kind; and the Korean boom was followed rapidly by a major recession. Moreover, social reactions to such fluctuations have changed since!

One conclusion from our second study is, again, that governments must avoid superficially convenient arrangements or devices — like the automatic tax claw-back from increased earnings, again — that now involve an implicit breach of the virtual consensus on which the mechanics of an equilibrium rate depend. In particular, it is dangerous to stability for governments to manipulate these arrangements for electoral purposes, or for political parties to promise to do so. In the context, this may be altogether too pious a prescription. But the 'political cycle' involves other aspects of economic policy than taxation; and for wages at least — towards which the studies suggested the policy of British governments to have been perceptibly affected by short-run political calculation — there would seem some possibility of insulating settlements from electoral considerations. One device which would appear (had it not in keeping politicians out allowed too many lawyers in) to offer a basis for that is the Australian Commonwealth system of wage determination: and though statutory compulsory arbitration might not be acceptable in countries with a different industrial relations tradition, one can conceive of alternative devices which would preserve the apparatus of independent collective bargaining but have something of the required effect — essentially, of keeping wage-policy out of politics.

This book's Introduction also indicates a number of measures which would moderate the degree of direct restraint, on wage-increases or on demand, required to keep inflation at a tolerable rate. If, as it suggested, the general labour supply curve (or Phillips Curve — the empirical validity of which the Introduction by implication supported) had been shifted by the development of unions, so that a given rate of general price-increase was now, in the long run and other things being equal, compatible only with a lower level of employment than previously, then it equally follows that a deliberate wage-policy is only one of several methods which might be employed (together) to shift the curve back to a more acceptable position. What the Introduction called 'Effects a, b and c' (in its Diagram B) indicate, for instance, measures to increase the facility with which 'secondary labour' (married women, older people, and so on) can enter or re-enter the labour market. They also suggest action to reduce the element of 'random search' for more suitable jobs which is implied in the tendency of voluntary labour turnover to rise at high employment levels — by better selection and induction procedures in employment, and by more adequate and positive employment information services. And policies to increase the mobility of skilled labour, and the ease of entry or transfer to expanding skilled and professional occupations are also implied. In sum, an 'Active Labour Market Policy' (to use the Swedish term) is important for inflation control, as well as for other reasons.

The most obvious international conclusion from our second study might well be that it would be exceedingly helpful, to national policies to control inflation, if the major industrial capitalist countries could at least agree to inflate at the same rate. But short of that, it is obviously better to try and arrange that necessary adjustments of international currency exchange rates take place by upward revaluations of strong currencies rather than by devaluations of weak ones.[1] The domestic effect of a devaluation on prices, income distribution and consequently wage-pressure is disturbing enough: but these effects may ultimately spread to other countries. In particular, again, the argument that the major adverse consequence of accelerated inflation is on the balance of payments, and that this can be harmlessly offset by repeated devaluations, flexible exchange rates or 'crawling pegs' is suspect. As our discussion of the strato-inflationary economies showed, such expedients provide a superficially facile adjustment of internal inflation to external trading relations. But the question is: adjustment into what?

Perhaps the most general and important conclusion from these studies is that, in 'pluralistic' societies at any rate, an effective policy to control inflation needs to pay a great deal of attention to social equity. And this is altogether too broad an issue to discuss in detail here — though it has many detailed aspects, some of which also involve problems that must be solved if (for instance) prevalent wage-systems and structures are not to be such as to make it probable that otherwise worthy attempts to raise productivity faster will increase cost inflation.[2] Supposing, however, that we are not satisfied with a mere confinement of inflation to the 'equilibrium rate' as a policy target, but prefer to aim at something more closely approaching price-stability proper — meaning a near-zero rate of change in the consumers' price level?

For such a target, the major consequence on which our first study can throw some light is for detailed price policy. That study (to repeat) suggested the centripetal path of normal or equilibrium inflations to have been defined by the tendency of wages in certain 'key' sectors of relatively fast productivity growth to rise as fast as productivity. From which it followed that the average rate of inflation was determined by the extent to which wages in other sectors, of slower productivity growth, could keep in line with the pace-setters. To revert to a diagrammatic technique of exposition, suppose that annual productivity growth in different 'sectors' of the economy ranges from a fast rate of about 7 per cent to a slow rate which is almost negligible (so that the average overall rate of rise in per capita output is for the economy as a whole about 3½ per cent; very close to the actual long-run average recently achieved by economies of diverse kinds). Then wages generally will tend, at least in a relatively integrated and organised condition of the labour market, to rise at the upper rate of about 7 per cent.

This situation is shown in the accompanying Diagram (a) as a 'fan' of lines representing the paths over time of productivity levels, with productivity growing at 7 per cent, 3½ per cent, and a negligible per cent, respectively in

---

(1) This is a point which the 'Shadow' British Prime Minister has well taken ("My Cure for Inflation", Mr. Harold Wilson, *The Sunday Times*, 6 Aug. 1972): all the more pity that he has also been sold on a variant of the penal tax on "excess" wage-increases.

(2) We hope to say something about these problems in a later *Occasional Paper* on the possibility and implications of a national job evaluation system.

(a) Equilibrium inflation: productivity and wages

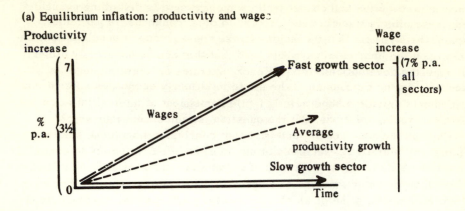

(b) Equilibrium inflation: wages and prices

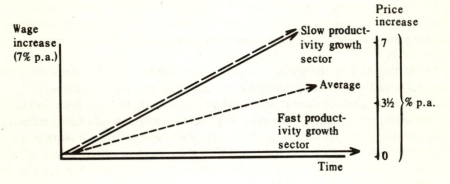

(c) Price stability: wage and price requirements

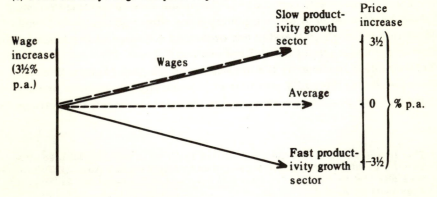

120

descending order. The path of wages in general is shown by a broken line, next to or possibly a little above[1] the path of productivity in the sector of fast productivity growth. This situation will, as we have already explained[2] cause a rise in prices. In each 'sector' the rise will (on the roughly reasonable assumption that increases in unit wage-costs are proportionately reflected in prices) correspond to the differences between the 'wages-path' and the 'productivity-path'. Using these, we can translate the wage-productivity differences of Diagram (*a*) into the 'price-paths' of Diagram (*b*). Again, we shall have a fan shape, with the 'price-path' in the sector of slowest productivity growth showing, naturally, the fastest increase. Individual product prices will change at *different* rates in the various sectors of the economy: prices in the fast productivity growth sector will be (approximately) stable; but in the sector of slow productivity growth they will increase at about 7 per cent a year.

The policy upshot can be indicated by Diagram (*c*): if the achievement of price stability involves average wages rising no faster than average productivity (i.e. at 3½ per cent annually again), then, with a similar translation of differences in 'wage-productivity paths' into 'price-paths', prices in the slow productivity growth sector will still rise at a 3½ per cent rate; so prices in the fast productivity growth sector must *decline* at the same rate to offset that effect. The 'fan' of wage-productivity-linked price dispersals in Diagram (*b*) must be swung downwards so that its spine, or average, approximates to the line of zero change, as in Diagram (*c*).

This diagrammatic representation is (like that of the Introduction) again not unrealistic. Table 1[†] shows the rate of change in prices in different consumption groups of the British and American consumers' price indices at consecutive periods. The table's analysis is, of course, rather crude: the dispersal of price-changes for *individual* commodities naturally extends over a much wider range than that of the last column; and the broader commodity groupings are not closely identical in the two indices. However, individual prices are also subject to variations arising from things like changing government indirect taxes or subsidies, and short-term market fluctuations; and the broad commodity groups have some rough correspondence to different productive sectors.

Generally speaking, the groups which show the lowest price increase in both indices consist in products – manufactures, invariably – of industries with a high productivity growth rate; while high rates of price increase are recorded in groups where the productivity growth rate is necessarily low – like public services and medical care. But the remarkable thing is that the dispersal of price increases between product groups should be quite independent of the differing overall rates of inflation displayed by the 'Total Index' for each national series at different periods: the American divergence is particularly consistent over time. Especially, neither the British nor the

---

(1) "Possibly a little above", to allow for an occasional effect of changes in international prices; see Equation (9), n. 1, p. 47, and preceding discussion.

(2) Equations (1) to (5), n. 1, p. 26, and preceding discussion.

United States divergence was significantly affected by the sharp acceleration of inflation in 1969—71.

Table 1[†]  *The dispersal of price increases* [a]

Average annual per cent increase in consumers' prices, for all commodities and for distinct groups

| | Total index | Highest commodity group | Lowest commodity group | Divergence between groups |
|---|---|---|---|---|
| *United Kingdom* | | | | |
| 1947—56 | 5.4 | 8.4 | 3.0 | 5.4 |
| 1956—62 | 2.0 | 4.4 | 0.3 | 4.1 |
| 1962—69 | 3.7 | 5.4 | 2.3 | 3.1 |
| 1969—71 | 7.9 | 10.9 | 5.9 | 3.0 |
| *United States* | | | | |
| 1947—52 | 3.5 | 4.5 | 1.5 | 3.0 |
| 1952—58 | 1.3 | 3.2 | 0.2 | 3.0 |
| 1958—69 | 2.2 | 4.1 | 0.5 | 3.5 |
| 1969—71 | 5.1 | 7.0 | 3.7 | 3.3 |

[a] This table simply updates one first used in another context (Turner, 'Collective Bargaining and the Eclipse of Incomes Policy...etc.' *loc. cit.*) by adding data for 1969—71. The 'groups' refer to the broader headings distinguished by national price indices — e.g. as 'food', 'household goods', 'transportation', etc. — and the periods distinguished are otherwise mainly those between important revisions in the indices, or which were originally relevant for other reasons. In the U.K. for 1969—71 the lowest group increase actually recorded was for 'tobacco' at 1.1% p.a.. But since over two-thirds of the price of tobacco products in Britain is Excise Duty, this was a temporary accident government tax policy, and the next lowest increase group (alcohol and clothing about tied for this place) was taken. It is, however, ironic that when the governmen has at last officially decided that smoking is a health risk, it should be fast makir it relatively cheaper.

To repeat, overall price stability means that actual prices over considerable sectors of the economy must come down. And neither the analysis of our first study nor the empirical observations of specialist economists suggest that to be an objective which can readily be attained by market processes alone. But even for a less ambitious target than that of absolute price-stability, this discussion of price-policy has considerable relevance. Thus, one expedient which governments have frequently resorted to as an inflation control is a 'price freeze'. The preceding analysis, however, implies that this will do little to restrain the central inflationary pressure which comes from high rates of wage-increase in fast productivity-growth sectors, because these sectors do not raise their prices much anyway. Its main effect will be on profits and wages in sectors where productivity growth is naturally slow, and this will produce distortions both in equity and the economy which may be explosively corrected when the price-freeze thaws. And if the price-freeze is accompanied by a wage-freeze, the consequent exceptional increase in profits in the fast-productivity growth sectors may induce the same effect.

Much the same consequences would follow from any prolonged attempt to enforce a general price-increase ceiling in the face of aggravated cost-inflation — like the notable (and rather noble) effort in the United Kingdom by the Confederation of British Industries in 1971/72. Insofar as the ceiling was effective — and the C.B.I.'s effort succeeded to a remarkable extent — its failure to discriminate between industries with different productivity trends would inevitably create distortions in *relative* rates of profit and wages. Such devices have some use as very temporary expedients, but unless they are followed up by measures to correct the distortions and inequities they themselves create, they involve large risks of aggravating inflation in the longer run.

From our second study, the most specific policy conclusions which arise are obviously for government fiscal policy. But in the British case, at least it is not clear that changes in government policy alone could totally eliminate 'orthodox' policy's hitherto aggravating effects on inflation. These were almost certainly made worse than they need have been, in the British case again, by the irregular character of the income-tax progression in the lower earnings rages — the sharp transition, from a nil deduction to an apparent marginal rate around 40 per cent, that followed from the abolition of the 'reduced rates' of tax which had previously cushioned entry into the tax net, and the absence of any further progression between that point of entry and the comparatively high income level at which super-tax became payable. Since the difference between the average and the marginal rate of tax was a key relation in the reactions our second study discussed, it would help if this difference were kept approximately constant (and if possible small) throughout the income range.

It would also help if there were some system by which the floor to the income-tax structure — the pay level at which tax became payable — were adjusted automatically by a figure corresponding to the general rise of incomes, and if it were publicly known that this adjustment would normally occur.[1] Ideally, this would be a proportion equivalent to the average increase in productivity on the assumption that average income in general will rise by this amount. However, even if governments were prepared to surrender the general advantage which the present annual accretion of a disproportionate tax yield gives them (in permitting the Chancellor of the Exchequer for instance, to play the role of periodic distributor of public largesse, or in allowing them to increase their own expenditure without ostensibly raising tax rates), it seems unlikely that they would agree to such an arrangement if the rise of incomes were in itself inflationary, since to do so would amount to an agreement to underwrite cost-inflation itself — or at least to make it painless to its participants.

(1) One gathers that in Holland something of this sort has recently been arranged; see O.E.C.D., *Economic Surveys: Netherlands*, 1970 and 1971.

On the other hand, the effects sketched in our second study, such as those in our *Example* of Table 21*, will operate even between annual budgets (and as we demonstrated in that connection, in the presence of rising incomes the effect of direct tax concessions on the average incidence of tax is relatively ephemeral). So that it seems equally unlikely that workers will again moderate their demands for additional income, unless there is some firm guarantee that this restraint will be adequately and regularly compensated in the budget itself.

The inference that incomes policy and taxation policy are not merely closely linked, but should be included in the same process of negotiation and agreement, is extended by another consideration. This is that the unions, too, are in a cleft stick. Again, the rate at which the real living standards of their members grow depends much more on government decision than on their own actions. For instance, in the years since 1959 covered by our Graph V* — which included the periods of two governments' incomes policies but also those of the most extensive strikes for wage-increases for fifty years — net real wages rose on average by 1.1 per cent annually.[1] In each of the three years excluded from the Graph (as affected by large tax concessions) net real wages rose by 3.1 per cent on average. And one could emphasise the point by a further calculation which is contained in Table 2†.

Table 2† *Changes in net real earnings (%) at various levels of income, 1970—73*
(married wage-earner with two children)

| April to April: | 1970—71 | | 1971—72 | | 1972—73 |
|---|---|---|---|---|---|
| Level of earnings | After 1970 Budget to before 1971 Budget | And after 1971 Budget | After 1971 Budget to before 1972 Budget | And after 1972 Budget | After 1972 Budget to before 1973 Budget |
| Highest decile | −1.0 | 0.3 | 3.6 | 5.8 | 1.5 |
| Median | −1.5 | 1.6 | 2.4 | 6.1 | 0.7 |
| Lowest decile | −1.0 | 2.7 | 1.6 | 6.7 | 0.1 |

The table contrasts the effect, granted the going schedules of taxation on earned income, of the money wage increases and price changes which took place in 1970—71 and 1970—72 between the April budgets, and the effect of the Budgets themselves. It also extends the calculations to an estimate for 1972—73, on the assumption (reasonable in the light of wage and price trends at time of writing) that average earnings will rise just over 9 per cent in that financial year, and prices just over 6 per cent.[2] It is quite clear that over the whole three years, wage-earners will have gained much more in real terms from the tax concessions of two Budgets than from nominal wage-increases.

(1) See p. 99.

(2) Otherwise, the estimate employs the data referred to in Section 3's Appendix B. If, however, the Aug. '72 *N.I.E.S.R. Economic Review* forecast (which follows the meteorologist's rule when in doubt, of predicting tomorrow's weather as the same as today's), that wages will rise at 12% and prices at up to 9%, should prove accurate, all the figures in the last column would become negative!

The median wage-earner, for example, gains only about one half per cent a year in terms of real disposable income, from direct wage increases (and most of that was probably an effect of the C.B.I.'s 'price-restraint' in 1971–72): but the two Budgets alone would have raised his real disposable income by over 2 per cent a year in the period. It is even more obvious that the distribution of real wage increases between workers at different levels of income was markedly changed by the two Budgets.

True, our second study also concludes that when governments are disinclined to co-operate fiscally in the raising of employee living standards, unions *can* increase real disposable wages by militant industrial action. But only at the cost of creating aggravated inequities amongst employees themselves, and particularly, of unemployment. A negotiated national wage and price policy which included an agreement on future taxation would therefore be in the wage-earners' own interest. But if such an agreement proves impossible to secure, is there no measure the unions themselves could take to improve matters, beyond a repeated resort to sectional militancy with all its adverse secondary and public consequences?

One possibility, of course, would be for them to negotiate price reductions instead of wage increases.[1] Given a marginal rate of tax on wages which exceeds the average rate (a necessary consequence of a progressive tax structure), a 2½ per cent reduction in prices would clearly represent a bigger increase in workers' real income than a 2½ per cent increase in nominal wages. This method, of course, suffers from the drawback that each union's negotiation with its own employer group would benefit other workers more than its own members. It would therefore require such a high degree of coordination in union policy that it would not be likely to be practicable except as a temporary or 'once-for-all' device — say, as a ploy in national bargaining over incomes and prices policy with the government. But from that point of view, the device suffers from a second disadvantage — that the government would benefit as much as, or more than, the unions' own members. To the extent that the government is also a purchaser of products from the non-governmental sector, its own costs would also decline, while its yield from direct taxation (at least) remained constant: so we should be back with almost the same problem of an automatic tendency for a budget surplus to emerge as exists under current wage and tax arrangements.

The only way the unions could avoid this would be for them to demand — in concert — both price reductions *and* wage-reductions. Curiously enough, this is also the only obvious way in which the trade union movement can raise workers' real living standards faster than productivity growth, without producing either inflation or a redistribution away from profits that might result in increased unemployment. The point can be simply demonstrated by using the same approximately (for Britain) realistic assumptions as in our *Illustration* of Table 19*, namely an average rate of tax on wages of 15 per

(1) A tactic once proposed by the late President of the United Automobile Workers' union in the U.S.A., Walter Reuther.

(2) See pp. 90–91.

cent and a marginal rate of 30 per cent. [2]  In that case, we showed that a
6½ per cent annual average wage increase had produced a rise in real
disposable wage-incomes per capita of less than 1 per cent a year. Suppose,
instead, that unions negotiate a general wage-*reduction* of 6½ per cent,
combined with a reduction in prices (to allow for the additional effect of our
assumed 2½ per cent yearly rise in British productivity) averaging 9 per cent,
It needs very little arithmetic to demonstrate that the fall in *net* cash wages
will be only 5⅓ per cent: which implies that real disposable earnings will
increase by some 4 per cent.

The difference over the normal increase of productivity, of course, would
in this case be supplied by a disproportionate reduction in the government's
tax yield — hopefully, even by a budget deficit. If we were operating under
current assumptions of excess capacity, no harm would be done, since
employment would be increased: it would, to say the least, be difficult for
the government to condemn the process as inflationary. While employers
should not object (provided some reasonable variation around the average
were arranged in the requisite price reductions, to allow for differences in
the natural rate of productivity growth in different sectors) because — unlike
the present scheme of things — the device would maintain their profits and
increase effective demand.

It is an irony of the contemporary industrial market economy, and its
characteristic fiscal arrangements, that within it unions in general can now
only both protect their members' employment and raise their members' real
living standards to match potential productive growth by largely abandoning
their traditional technique of separate bargaining with employers for wage
increases. If they cannot bargain, centrally, with the government instead, their
logical alternative is to reverse their historical demand for more money, and
press for price *and* wage reductions as a means to higher real income!

University of Cambridge Department of Applied Economics
Occasional Papers